Sir John Templeton

FROM WALL STREET
TO HUMILITY THEOLOGY

Sir John Templeton

FROM WALL STREET
TO HUMILITY THEOLOGY

Robert L. Herrmann

TEMPLETON FOUNDATION PRESS

Philadelphia & London

TEMPLETON FOUNDATION PRESS
Five Radnor Corporate Center, Suite 120
100 Matsonford Road
Radnor, Pennsylvania 19087

Printed in the United States of America

Library of Congress Cataloging-in-Publication Data

Herrmann, Robert L., 1928-
    Sir John Templeton : from Wall Street to humility theology /
Robert L. Herrmann.
        p.   cm.
    Includes bibliographical references and index.
    ISBN 1-890151-27-0
    1.   Templeton, John, 1912-   . 2. Capitalists and financiers—
United States—Biography.   3. Philanthropists—United States—
Biography.   4. Christian biography.   5. Humility—Christianity.
I. Title.
HG172.H474   1998
332.6'092—dc21
    [B]   98-13823
                                                                  CIP

Contents

Part I

THE BENEFITS OF INVESTING
IN HUMILITY THEOLOGY SCIENCE

Part II

 THE MAKING OF A
WORLD-CLASS INVESTOR

Appendixes

Preface

This book chronicles the life of a man of extraordinary vision. John Templeton set the pace on Wall Street with an astounding record of mutual fund achievement, and also startled his contemporaries with his keen insights about market forces and his optimism about the growth of the economy. But John Templeton has made the real goal of his life the elaboration of a new concept of spiritual progress. While recognizing and appreciating the great religious insights of the past, he envisions a new era of spiritual discovery that may rival the astounding physical discoveries of the past few centuries brought to us through science.

It was an honor to be asked to write John's biography, and, in doing so, I have relied heavily upon our fifteen-year association. During this time we have written two books together, *The God Who Would Be Known* and *Is God the Only Reality?* and I have assisted him in the editing of a number of others. I was also privileged to be a charter member of the John Templeton Foundation board of trustees, along with Sir John, Lady Irene, their son Jack Templeton, and Scottish theologian Thomas Torrance.

In order to work on this book over the past two years, I have been fortunate enough to have had relief from some of my administrative duties with the two major Templeton Foundation projects I direct through Gordon College. Professors Jack Haas and Harold Heie have provided tremendous help with the Science & Religion Course Program and Patsy Ames has been indispensable as managing editor of *Progress in Theology,* the humility theology newsletter that I have edited for the Foundation for the past five years. I am also grateful for the day-to-day support and wisdom provided by my administrative assistant, Rebecca Keefe, and my secretary, Alyson Lindsay. Above all I am grateful to my wife, Betty, whose critique, encouragement, and word processing skills have made this book a reality.

Robert L. Herrmann

Sir John Templeton

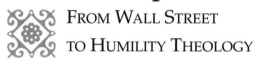 FROM WALL STREET
TO HUMILITY THEOLOGY

Introduction

Sir John Marks Templeton celebrated his eightieth birthday with a great gathering of family and friends on November 29, 1992 at the Union League of Philadelphia. I was privileged to be there and to give the invocation, though I am not a "man of the cloth" but only a biochemist who happens to be a Christian and co-author with Sir John of two of his many books. Writing the biography of a man with so many accomplishments is a truly daunting task, and whenever I forget how enormous the assignment, I just think back to that joyous night in Philadelphia. The list of attendees would easily pass for a random excerpt from *Who's Who in America* and *Who's Who in the World*. The variety of accents emphasized the global nature of Sir John's relationships: Jewel Templeton, brother Harvey Templeton's effervescent wife with the delightful twang of the Tennessee mountains; the British Sir Sigmund Sternberg from London; Irish-born Reverend Wilbert Forker, administrator of the Templeton Prize for Progress in Religion; Mena Griffiths, Sir John's private secretary of twenty-five years in Nassau, Bahamas; and Wyoming State Senator Gail Zimmerman, spouse of daughter Anne Templeton Zimmerman, to name a few.

At the time of this writing, Sir John is nearing his eighty-fifth birthday, yet it is the considered opinion of many of his friends that he remains one of the youngest, most forward-thinking, incisive, and progressive investors of the twentieth century. That may seem an odd description for a man who left the world of stocks and bonds in 1992, selling his $25 billion group of Templeton Funds to Franklin Resources, Inc., but the truth is that Sir John has another investment program under way, one that he hopes will rival the staggering $10 billion per week the world now invests in scientific research. It is an investment in the spiritual development of human beings! As Sir John expresses it, "The enormous impact of scientific discovery on our physical lives and on our beginnings of an understanding of our place in the universe can show us how to achieve rapid progress in obtaining spiritual information, including information about the Unlimited Creative Spirit, in which we live and move and have our being." The benefits, he believes, would be staggering. As he said in a recent lecture at Templeton College, Oxford University,

> Unfortunately, too often people focus on the negatives and lose sight of the multitude of blessings that surround us and the limitless potential that exists for the future. The beneficial effects of religion on our attitudes, our motivations, our interactions with people, our goals, and our basic well-being can be of immeasurable value.

Sir John believes the limitless potential of religion needs to be unlocked. The traditional religions have brought us wonderful and powerful insights and a legacy in sacred art and music, but in recent centuries they have produced little that could be called progress in spiritual information. One solution, he believes, lies in the application of the scientific method, so familiar to us in this age, to the cause of progress in religion. The billions spent on medical research—largely concerned with our physical and mental well-being—have brought us many miraculous cures and greatly increased longevity. Deaths from diseases like tuberculosis, typhoid fever, diphtheria, syphilis, pneumonia, polio, and cholera are now only a tiny fraction of what they were fifty years ago. Infant mortality has dropped sharply and longevity has increased greatly. Indeed, it has been estimated that 65 percent of all the people who ever lived beyond age sixty-five are alive today.

Furthermore, the impact that scientific research has had on our health shows every promise of intensifying, for it is estimated that 50 percent of all that is known in medicine has been discovered in just the last fifteen years and 90 percent in the present century.

By contrast, the traditional religions have been largely backward-looking, and the newer mystical religious movements of our day are often superstitious and unscientific. What may be needed, John Templeton says, is a new dynamic, empirical, scientific approach to investigation of spiritual phenomena carried out by those trained in the scientific approach and aware of the complexities of scientific interpretation. Furthermore, many of the current discoveries in fields like physics, cosmology, molecular biology, and neural science strongly suggest questions of a philosophical and theological nature, pointing to a great potential in these areas for new spiritual understanding and research. The power of science has been awesome, but even science seems to point beyond itself to a deeper, spiritual meaning!

There is fascination and even a hint of irony in the fact that John Templeton has made progress in religion the great goal of his life. For even though he was raised in a home where religion was taken quite seriously he often expressed the conviction that his gifts did not lie in the Christian ministry. Instead, because of a habit of thrift and the appreciation for a good investment—strong influences from both his parents—he trained in economics at Yale and law at Oxford and became a part of the then new field of investment counseling. Actually, Sir John chose investing in part with the idea that he might make a financial contribution to progress in Christian ministry. And indeed, that intention has been realized on the grand scale for the benefit of a large number of church organizations, the most notable being Princeton Theological Seminary, where he served for many years as chairman of the board. As head of the financial committee he helped multiply the school's endowment one hundred-fold. And John Templeton is now claiming new ground in the field of philanthropy. For his approach goes beyond the mere "do-goodism" of ordinary philanthropy to express a deep sense of stewardship, a commitment to use the rewards of his gift as an investor to promote the moral and spiritual progress of mankind. What better *ministry* could one have?!

But one might ask if the goal of progress in religion is really attainable. Sir John's answer is to point again at the remarkable progress in so many areas of our lives. Recently, at a lecture in Oxford, he said that we live in a period of prosperity never seen before in world history. In America, the gross national product is thirty times what it was just fifty years ago. The average hourly wage of a factory worker has increased in real terms by over 65 percent. Today, America has more than 3.5 million families with assets over 1 million dollars and worldwide there are over 400 billionaires. He went on to say,

> If you look further back to when Adam Smith wrote his great book called *An Inquiry into the Nature and Causes of the Wealth of Nations* you will see that 85 percent of the world's population had to work in agriculture just to produce enough food. Today, less than 4 percent work on farms in America and they produce great surpluses. Dire predictions that farming output would be unable to meet the needs of a rapidly expanding population failed to account for the incredible productivity gains that have occurred. In the last thirty years, improvements in crop varieties, pesticides, and fertilizers have helped *triple* agricultural productivity. This has saved the clearing of forests equal in area roughly to the size of North America, which additional acreage would have been needed for

increased food supply. New methods such as high yield and no-till farming hold promise for continued improvements around the world.

Since the time of Adam Smith's writing, the yearly production of goods and services has increased *one hundred-fold.* In fact, more than half the goods produced in history have been produced just in the latest two hundred years. Before Adam Smith, there were fewer than one thousand corporations on earth. Today, corporations are being created at the rate of *two thousand* in the U.S. every business day. Underlying this growth is the increasing acceptance of the importance of *free* trade and *enterprise* within and among nations. The trend toward greater free market economics accelerated in the early 1980s as the number of privatizations began to outpace nationalizations. Privatizations of state-owned enterprises around the world have soared from less than *$10 billion* in 1985 to more than *$300 billion* in 1992 as the failures of socialism have grown increasingly obvious and unbearable.

The trend toward greater capitalism unleashes tremendous potential for efficiency gains and greater wealth potential. So does the shift away from regulation and autarchy toward free trade. World *exports* today in real dollar terms are more than *eleven times* what they were just forty years ago. Numerous institutions have arisen to protect the principles that have fostered this dramatic growth and to spread the preconditions necessary for ongoing free trade throughout the world. Consider this: Just fifty years ago, there was no General Agreement on Tariffs and Trade, no Organization for Economic Cooperation and Development, no United Nations, no World Bank, no Organization of American States, no International Monetary Fund, no European Economic Community, and no North American Free Trade Agreement.

The *new* International Monetary Fund revisions also indicate that the world output is growing *faster* that we had realized—over 20 percent faster in fact. Standards of living in some of the developing countries are rising 8 percent yearly on average. As income levels rise, so will consumer spending, creating new opportunities not only for local businesses but also for companies in industrialized countries, which will find massive new marketplaces opening up for their products. In India, for example, the middle class is estimated to be equal in size to more than the entire population of the United Kingdom and is growing at a rate of 20 percent a year.

Sir John also tells us that technologically, we have seen incredible progress. Fiber optics allows for transmission of eight thousand conversations as compared with forty-eight on the old copper wire. In 1940 there were no VCRs, no computers, no photocopiers, no compact discs, no microprocessors, no man-made satellites, no fax machines, no modems, no answering machines, no Internet. More than half the books ever written were written since 1940 and more than twenty-five times as much is spent on research and development. There are also four times as many scientists and engineers.

More than half the discoveries in natural science have been made during the twentieth century. Authors John Naisbitt and Patricia Aburdene, writing in *Megatrends 2000*, told us that the amount of information available is doubling every two and a half years. At that rate, there will be one thousand times as much information available in the next twenty-five years. In 1950, 17 percent of the American population worked in information-related occupations. In 1982 this number had risen to 65 percent. The significance of this continuing information explosion cannot be overemphasized. Sir John says:

> Perhaps the most significant implication this information revolution holds for the future stems from its seemingly infinite nature. Our economic prosperity is no longer primarily a function of *limited natural* resources but is becoming progressively more heavily dependent on the self-perpetuating, *limitless* body of knowledge. This bodes well for a continuation and acceleration of the underlying trend toward prosperity that has blessed mankind in this century. . . . The more we are able to take advantage of the information explosion around us, the more we are able to liberate our minds from routine tasks and to cultivate high degrees of analytical thinking, the greater the prosperity with which we will be rewarded.

These momentous developments in the world economy and in technology lead Sir John to the conviction that we may be poised for a similar revolution in spiritual knowledge. Progress in additional new spiritual information is not only possible, but given these examples of advancement in our physical and intellectual lives, progress is the logical development for our spiritual nature as creatures of the Unlimited Creative Spirit.

The main barrier to our full flowering as spiritual beings, Sir John says, is human egotism. It has been our great sin as God's creatures to assume far more knowledge than we actually possess. Indeed, our successes in the worlds of economics and technology can easily give rise to a Promethean attitude, in which we are unteachable and self-satisfied. But the scientific approach, which has made all of this wondrous development possible, has, especially in this past generation, brought us to a place of acute awareness of how infinitesimal we are in the cosmic scheme of things. The end result, John Templeton says, should be a feeling of humility toward the Creator and an eagerness to learn. This awareness, this searching experience directed toward the God of the universe, he has called "humility theology."

So convinced is Sir John of the necessity for this humility toward God that he has built a major focus of his goal of progress in religion around this idea. He has also organized a Humility Theology Information Center within the Tennessee-based John Templeton Foundation, first organized in 1987, and brought together a distinguished group of scientists and theologians to form an advisory board. It is this organization to which Sir John looks for advice and for participation in programs he is developing to promote progress in religion. Descriptions of some of these programs will form some of the later chapters in this book. They include programs to stimulate the teaching of university courses in science and religion, worldwide lecture programs organized around the concept of humility theology, and prizes for articles on humility theology published in science and religion journals.

Another exciting initiative involves high school students in Sir John's own Franklin County, Tennessee. Essay contests begun there several years ago offer prizes for essays on a student's own choice of moral or spiritual principles to live by. The most recent competition involved over eight hundred entries, and winners were recognized at a country club banquet, in newspaper articles, and with cash prizes of as much as two thousand dollars. The Foundation is involved in a large expansion of this program to communities worldwide. Other programs include an in-depth study of spiritual factors in health and a program for medical schools to encourage the teaching of courses integrating medical science and religion.

The forerunner of these many new initiatives by the Humility Theology Information Center is the Templeton Prize for Progress in Religion, a program John Templeton began with an award to Mother Teresa of Calcutta in 1973. The prize has been awarded every year since then, the amount of the prize being always slightly larger than the various Nobel Prizes, to signify Sir John's feeling that progress in religion is the most important goal of all.

All of these activities are a source of great personal joy and expectation for John Templeton. One could sense his excitement and pleasure at a recent meeting of the advisory board when he said to the some thirty-five board members and Foundation staff assembled at Unity Village, Missouri, "I want to tell you what great enthusiasm I feel for what we are doing and I hope you too are full of enthusiasm and joy."

He is clearly quite optimistic about these plans and about this group of advisors and staff members, which is not surprising given that optimism has been a hallmark of John Templeton since early childhood. This attitude developed partly because of a remarkable sense of self-assurance, and partly because of a belief that his mother, as a devoted follower of the Unity School of Christianity, had instilled in him

very early in his life. She taught him that God wanted our material prosperity and provided for us an inner strength and
wisdom, a kind of divine spark, which would enable us to
prosper materially as a natural consequence of intelligent
planning and spiritual preparation, especially as we seek to
help and love everyone.

John Templeton has followed the principle of opening
every board meeting of his Global Fund meetings—as well
as any other meetings where he was in charge—with
prayer, thanking God for multiple blessings and opportunities. I recall one special occasion, in 1984, when my wife and
I attended the dedication of Templeton College in Oxford,
England. The audience was a prestigious one, and those on
the platform included the minister of education of the United
Kingdom and the chancellor of Oxford University—complete
with his starched Elizabethan collar—and various other
school officials and community dignitaries. At the end, Sir
John made his address, dedicating the college to the memory
of his parents and then concluding with an expression of deep
thankfulness to God for the many blessings that had been
poured out upon everyone attending, but especially for the
blessing of his own parents and his associates in the development of the college. I recall the look of surprise on the faces of
many of the academics as God was acknowledged, and I was
proud that John had shown his appreciation for the true
source of Templeton College or any other institution put together with human hands but ultimately an expression of the
Creator's love and generosity.

For John Templeton, optimism and gratitude go hand in
hand. During an interview on the Canadian Television program *Cross Currents*, he said of his philanthropy that he did
not inherit his wealth, but that at the time of his marriage to
Judith Folk, they began a pattern of saving in which they
pledged half of their income to the church and investment.
This led to a game of bargain-hunting, budget control, and
careful investment, which provided the foundation for his

wealth. Coupled with this lifestyle of thrift and saving was a desire he had been given from early childhood to help others, and he suggested that this willingness to be helpful and useful was actually a source of optimism, just as optimism was a basis for being helpful and useful. As he said, "The two go hand in hand." And then he added some thoughts about gratitude:

> Thanksgiving and gratitude will revolutionize your life. If you wake up every day and think of five new things that you are overwhelmingly grateful for, your day will go better, people will like you better, you'll be more successful. Try it! A girl said to me once, "I can't think of anything to *be* thankful for." So I said, "Just stop breathing for three minutes and you'll be very thankful you can breathe again."

Optimism and thankfulness have certainly characterized John Templeton's career, but they have always been accompanied by serious attention to in-depth study and thorough preparation. "Is it cost-effective?" is one of his favorite responses.

As we look to his many new investment programs for the encouragement of spiritual progress, we recall the stupendous results of his careful preparation and persevering optimism in the past. Those of us working with him in these new endeavors are learning the lessons that have been so productive for him throughout the past years. After all, who can question the effectiveness of the Templeton Growth Fund? An investment of $10,000 in the fund in November of 1954 was worth $3 million forty-three years later if dividends were reinvested. And, as Sir John points out, that was a gain in material benefits. Who can estimate the gain on an investment in the largely untapped spiritual potential of mankind? John Templeton believes it could dwarf even that global fund in its fruitfulness!

Part I

 THE BENEFITS OF INVESTING IN
HUMILITY THEOLOGY SCIENCE

CHAPTER 1

An Investment in Scientific Research for More Spiritual Knowledge

 In the view of John Templeton, progress in spiritual information is not only possible, but may be a consequence of God's creative role in our evolutionary history. Ours is a fascinating pilgrimage, starting slowly with the crude awakenings in our early ancestors, who sometimes buried their dead with food and implements for a next world, following through the flourishing of Druids and Mayans and Egyptians, who left to their gods their curious monuments and exquisite pyramids, then on to the great mystics of India and the Middle East who left us the Vedas, the Holy Bible, and the Koran as well as majestic cathedrals and temples. And now, it would seem that our fascination with the meaning of our existence grows deeper and more powerful, a perhaps surprising phenomenon in a scientific age where some thought science would have explained away religion.

The prior periods of human evolutionary history emphasized our physical and intellectual development; brain size more than doubled in contrast to earlier species and we learned to walk upright and use our hands skillfully. The exquisitely painted caves of Europe are evidence of just how skilled our ancestors were! And the current rate of acceleration of our intellectual development is phenomenal. Technologically, as Sir John told us in his 1995 Templeton College lecture, our progress is astounding. In the past fifty years we have written as many books as were written in all of previous human history, and over half of the discoveries in the sciences have been made in our century.

Sir John sees our rate of spiritual development as only now beginning to accelerate, just as there were periods of gradual growth followed by rapid development in the physical and intellectual periods over the two hundred thousand years of our history as a species. However, the rapid changes currently occurring in the intellectual phase, especially in the sciences, have introduced for Sir John a radically new vision of our place in the cosmos and set the stage for a giant leap forward in our spiritual understanding, a second Renaissance.

Many of these recent discoveries in fields such as physics, cosmology, neural science, and evolutionary biology have been so mind-boggling that they have changed the very way we think of ourselves and of our place in the universe. Certainly they have brought many of the practitioners—the scientists themselves—to a state of wonderment and humility, and provoked their serious consideration of philosophical and theological questions.

In an earlier book, *The God Who Would Be Known,* Sir John and I talked about the spirituality of humankind.

> Humanity's fascination with a spiritual dimension, a hidden sphere of power, an underlying ordering principle that lies unseen behind everyday events as well as gigantic happenings, has grown and taken on new importance in the ensuing centuries. Science has given us knowledge of the fundamental structure of matter in terms of a plethora of subatomic particles, and knowledge of processes of biology in terms of molecular mechanisms. But each new explanation seems to open up deeper questions, as though we still see only the outline of things and explain our observations by means of models that only approximate the truth. Indeed, many in science now see the limitations of scientific description and do not presume that scientific descriptions are ultimate truth. For some there is

the added conviction that the Creator is revealing himself through science, so that the results of science serve as signs pointing to a larger Reality.[1]

Among the scientific discoveries displaying this philosophic, searching character we would include the current evidence for the Big Bang, a gigantic explosion which appears to have generated our cosmos as well as both time and space some 15 billion years ago. The products of this grand synthesis, star systems of enormous proportions, number in the hundreds of billions. The numbers are so large that there is no simple analogy to help our minds to take it in. Someone has said that the number of stars is roughly equivalent to all the grains of sand on all the beaches in the world! Timothy Ferris has addressed the question of size in his book, *Coming of Age in the Milky Way.* He says:

> And yet the more we know about the universe, the more we come to see how little we know. When the cosmos was thought to be but a tidy garden, with the sky its ceiling and earth its floor and its history coextensive with that of the human family tree, it was still possible to imagine that we might one day comprehend it in both plan and detail. That illusion can no longer be sustained. We might eventually obtain some sort of bedrock understanding of cosmic structure, but we will never understand the universe in detail; it is just too big and varied for that. If we possessed an atlas of our galaxy that devoted but a single page to each star system in the Milky Way (so that the sun and all its planets were crammed on one page), that atlas would run to more than ten million volumes of ten thousand pages each. It would take a library the size of Harvard's to house the atlas, and merely to flip through it, at the rate of a page per second, would require over ten thousand years. Add the details of planetary cartography, potential extraterrestrial biology, the subtleties of scientific principles involved, and the historical dimensions of change, and it becomes clear that we are never going to learn more than a tiny fraction of the story of our galaxy alone—and there are

a hundred billion more galaxies. As the physician Lewis Thomas writes, "The greatest of all the accomplishments of twentieth-century science has been the discovery of human ignorance."[2]

This humbling realization is only one of the most recent occurrences. If we move from astronomy to physics, we are confronted with such things as the strange behavior of the elementary particles of matter, which sometimes display the character of particles and sometimes behave instead like waves. Then, too, there appears to be a built-in limitation in the accuracy of our observation of these elementary particles, a phenomenon Werner Heisenberg called the uncertainty principle. The upshot of this measurement limitation is that we cannot know simultaneously both the position and the momentum of such particles; if we know where the particle is, we don't know where it's going, and if we know where it's going, we don't know where it is!

Sir John anticipated much of what we see now as the significance of these and many other strange and wondrous observations from the sciences. In his earlier book, *The Humble Approach*, written in 1981, he spoke of this new revelation of God from the "vast unseen."

Some people think supernatural events, such as miracles, are needed to prove God's existence. But natural processes and the laws of nature may be merely methods designed by God for His continuing creative purposes. When new laws are discovered by human scientists, do they not merely discover a little more of God?

Each of us every day is swimming in an ocean of unseen miracles. For example, each living cell is a miracle; and the human body is a vast colony of over a hundred billion cells. The miracle of this body includes both our ability to recognize it as well as our inability ever to exhaust the true significance of it. As Albert Einstein said, "The most incomprehensible thing about the universe is that it is comprehensible." That the universe exhibits order, not chaos, suggests the futility of trying to fathom the nature of matter without investigating the unseen spirit behind it. Each time new laws are discovered by scientists, however, we learn a little more about God and the ways He continually maintains and is building His creation.

A mythical observer from another universe, who might have witnessed the spectacular Big Bang when the universe was created about eighteen billion years ago, would have seen after the first year only a vast blackness with thin clouds of stars and other fragments flying apart. But we, who observe from the surface of our small planet earth, see a totally different picture. We see a drama of evolution and progress on the surface of our earth, which is truly amazing and miraculous. And this progress is speeding up faster and faster and faster. By an unbelievable miracle, billions of humans, each of whom is a colony of billions of atoms, have suddenly covered the face of the earth. Most amazing of all is the fact that the unseen minds of these humans are accumulating knowledge in explosive proportions—knowledge of themselves, the universe, of their Creator. Could we ever make an observer from another universe believe this unseen explosion of human knowledge really exists? Would we believe that these new invisible minds are themselves participating creators in the ongoing drama of evolutionary creation?[3]

These, then, are the kinds of scientific data that convince John Templeton that we are on the threshold of great discoveries of spiritual information. But, as we said in the Introduction, he does not believe the leap forward will occur without a change in the hearts of the inquirers.

Sir John feels that a great barrier to our full flowering as spiritual beings is human egotism. Admittedly, there is much to be proud of, and our science and technology has brought us wondrous and often needful things, but we have forgotten the source. We assume far more knowledge and ability than we possess. We have forgotten Lewis Thomas's conclusion that this is the Age of Ignorance. And what we are *most* ignorant of is the Creator. It is humility toward the Creator that Sir John is concerned about!

In *The Humble Approach*, Sir John writes of a new approach to understanding more about God. His method consists of a broad, sweeping examination of our sources of theological knowledge from the various religions and from modern sources in the sciences, followed by proposals for research for spiritual progress. The essential ingredient for success, he says, is a humble approach.

> The word humility is used here to mean admission that God infinitely exceeds anything anyone has ever said of Him; and that He is infinitely beyond human comprehension and understanding. A prime purpose of this book is to help us become more humble and thereby reduce the stumbling blocks placed in our paths toward heaven by our own egos. If the word heaven means eternal peace and joy, then we can observe that some persons have more of it already than others. Have you observed that these are generally persons who have reduced their egos, those who desire to give rather than to get? The Holy Spirit seems to enter when invited and to dwell with those who try to surrender to Him their hearts and minds. "Behold, I stand at the door and knock; if any man hear my voice and open the door, I will come in to him and sup with him, and he with me" (Revelation 3:20 KJB). As men grow older and wiser, they often grow in humility.
>
> The humble approach has much in common with but is not the same as natural theology, process theology, or empirical theology, whose horizons are all too narrow. They often attempt to give a comprehensive or systematic picture of God in keeping with human observations. But the humble approach teaches that man can discover and comprehend only a few of the infinite aspects of God's nature, never enough to form a comprehensive theology. The humble approach may be a science still in its infancy, but it seeks to develop a way of knowing God appropriate to His greatness and our littleness. The humble approach is a search which looks forward, not backward and which expects to grow and learn from its mistakes.
>
> All of nature reveals something of the Creator. That golden age of creation is reached as the Creator reveals Himself more and more to the minds of men. Man cannot learn all about God, the Creator, by studying nature because nature is only a contingent and partial manifestation of God. Hence

natural theology, which seeks to learn about God through nature, is limited. Recently a new concept of theology, called the theology of science, was born. It denotes the way in which natural scientists are meditating about the Creator on the grounds of their observations of the astronomic and subatomic domains, but also on the grounds of investigations into living organisms and their evolution, and such invisible realities as the human mind.

Experimental theology can reveal only a very little about God. It begins with a few simple forms of inquiry, subject to little disagreement, and proceeds to probe more deeply in thousands of other ways. Spiritual realities are not quantifiable of course, but there may be aspects of spiritual life that can be demonstrated experimentally one by one even though there be hundreds of failures for each success. This approach is similar to that of experimental medicine.

As with experimental theology, the humble approach implies that there is a growing body of knowledge and an evolving theology not limited to any one nation or cultural area. The truly humble should be so open-minded that they welcome religious views from any place in the universe that is peopled with intelligent life. Seekers following the humble approach are never so xenophobic that they reject ideas from other nations, religions, or eras. Because the humble approach to theology is ongoing and constantly evolving, it may never become obsolete.

When learning about God, a worldwide approach is much too small. Even a universe-wide approach is much too small. The "picture" 99 percent of people have of God is too small. Have you heard anyone say, "God is a part of life"? Would it not be wiser to say of humanity that it is only an infinitesimal speck of all that has its being in and through God? Our own ego can make us think that we are the center rather than merely one tiny temporal outward manifestation of a vast universe of being, which subsists in the eternal and infinite reality that is God. Have you heard the words, "the realm of the Spirit"? Is there any other realm? Humanity on this little earth may be an aspect of all that is upheld by the Spirit, but the Spirit is not an "aspect" of humanity. To say that God is a "part" or an "aspect" of life is as blind as for a man, standing on a shore looking at a wave, to say, "The ocean is an aspect of that wave."[4]

Sir John anticipated much of what is happening and needs to take place today in the theological world, just as his investment strategies of the Templeton Investment Funds era showed a keen sense of analysis and a willingness to speculate responsibly but in the broadest international context. In the true spirit of humility, he calls for a strategy, which has served so well for the sciences but is so foreign in theology, of examining every possibility with a willingness to accept truth wherever it is found, and to continually test and re-examine what has been passed down from before and what has been accepted in the present.

Admittedly, this is a tall order for theology, which operates from the standpoint of revelation and knows little of the empirical methods of the sciences. In fact, major religions are only now coming out of a deliberate separation from the scientific world, led by some of theology's most eminent scholars. Theologian Ronald Cole-Turner has reminded us that the church moved into a period of isolation from science and technology some fifty years ago through the leadership of theologians like Karl Barth and later Langdon Gilkey. Religion's rejection of science as a resource for theology contained one primary advantage: religion was insulated from the misuse of science and from the disturbing theories of science that could be interpreted to explain away the uniqueness of human beings and human consciousness. The fallacy of this approach, which Gilkey has since admitted, is seen in the almost total isolation of religious values from our culture. Cole-Turner describes this failure and the desirability for a new engagement with science and technology:

> The disadvantage is that this strategy alienates theology not only from science but from the natural world itself. If the scientific interpretation of nature has no implications for

Christianity, then Christian interpretation of creation has no consequences for science's understanding of nature. Skeptics quickly asked whether Christianity had any consequences at all. Was it nothing but a set of stories intended to motivate good behavior? Or was it an isolated language game, a way Christians talk in church but untranslatable into the common speech of the broader culture? Christianity was no longer taken seriously because it made no claim. It was simply God-talk, empty and irrelevant to life in the world.

Now, however, science and technology have permeated our whole conceptual universe, even redefining human consciousness. Our theology has been pushed off the conceptual map of contemporary thought, leaving science with its largely unchallenged reductionistic assumptions to define our existence. Our strategy of isolation must end, and our Christian convictions must be brought into an honest engagement with science and technology. Thus transformed, our theology can seek to transform this culture of science and technology. Then our theology and ethics might join with our science and technology in a new alliance to search for the future of humanity God intends.[5]

John Templeton is also eager for a "transformed theology," but with less emphasis on problem solving and more concern for a humble spirit and an open mind. Again in *The Humble Approach* he says:

There are clear scriptural bases for advocating the need for an inquiring and open mind. According to St. Luke, Jesus said, "Ask, and it shall be given you; seek, and you shall find; knock, and it shall be opened unto you. For everyone who asks, receives, and he who seeks, finds; and to him who knocks it shall be opened" (Luke 11:9–10, New American Standard). Maybe God reveals Himself where He finds an inquiring mind—an open mind.

In the Acts of the Apostles St. Paul said, "The God who made the world and everything in it . . . made from one every nation of men . . . that they should seek God, in the hope that they might feel after Him and find Him. Yet He is not far from each of us, for "In Him we live and move and have our being"; as even some of your poets have said, "For we are indeed His offspring" (Acts 17:24–28, NAS).

Christ came to reveal God to men. But because of the limitations of human minds and human language, maybe less than one-hundredth part has been handed down to us. It is easy for us to realize how ignorant and primitive were the Jews of two thousand years ago and the Hindus of three thousand years ago. We should be humble enough to admit that if they had only perhaps one-tenth of one percent of all knowledge, we may have only one percent, even though the little glimpses we do have are indeed awesome.

One following the humble approach thinks it possible that God may want to reveal Himself further than He has done to date in any major or minor religion. He may be ever ready to give us new revelation if we will but open our minds to seek and inquire, but first we must rid ourselves of that rigidity and intellectual arrogance that tells us we have all the answers already. Like natural scientists who already assume the humble approach in their studies, maybe we should recognize that the law of creation is a law of accelerating change. Human language has always been too inadequate and restricted to utter all truths once and for all. The human mind has never been ready to receive all knowledge.

Time, space, and energy are the limits of our lives as they are the limits of our knowledge. God, of course, is not bound in these ways. He is the Creator of the awesome vastness of His cosmos. He knows each person's most fleeting thought just as He knows the power of a quasar and the intricate complexity of a DNA molecule. His most marvelous and mysterious creation on earth is the human brain with its indwelling mind. With the use of our minds, we can participate in some small ways in the creation of matter and even life itself. It should be clear to us that even though we are seriously hampered by our human weaknesses, we are means to share with God his readiness to reveal Himself to us. We have a duty of humility, the duty to be open-minded.[6]

This, then, is the foundation upon which John Templeton's spiritual investment program is proceeding. Since 1987, the ideas he has proposed have been formalized as major programs of the John Templeton Foundation with the words "humility theology" to signify the goal of a new attitude of humility toward the Creator God on the part of the theological community. Implied also is the importance of openness to the discoveries of current science; most recently Sir John has suggested that our goal should be a new science in which additional spiritual knowledge is sought by the empirical and statistical methods of science. He has called this new goal "humility theology science."

CHAPTER 2

Research on Spiritual Characteristics

The Laws of the Spirit

Sir John has had a strong interest in the study of what he calls spiritual laws, universal principles governing spiritual growth and development, which reflect God's purpose in bringing about change, process, and progress in His creation. It is, Sir John says in the 1995 edition of *The Humble Approach*, a research area of tremendous need and great opportunities.

> By "laws of the spirit" we mean universal principles of the unseen world that can be determined and tested by extensive examination of human behavior and other data. Partly for lack of clearly defined methodology and a body of research material, this field appears about as disorganized and controversial as the natural sciences were in the millenniums before Galileo. In the days of Moses or Mohammed, there was very little knowledge of the principles of physics, chemistry, or biology, and little appreciation among the average people of the progress and rich rewards that could be achieved through successful research in these fields.
>
> Just as people of earlier times were ignorant regarding the physical sciences, we today are ignorant about the principles of spiritual progress. In addition to having as yet little understanding or agreement as to what spiritual laws are, we do not seem to recognize that God's purpose is not some

permanent status quo, but change, process, and progress based upon the laws of the spirit. The spiritual dimensions of the cosmos are dynamic, changing, ceaselessly interacting. Surely the time has come for us to concentrate our resources on the kind of investigations that will enable us to understand the patterns and laws governing spiritual growth and development. Ceaseless seeking may be a part of the growth of souls as well as minds. It may be possible through research that some agreement may be reached on laws of the spirit. This field of research may yet become as bounteously fruitful as the natural sciences were in the last four centuries. . . .

Of course, it is not very apparent at this moment in history exactly how each law of the spirit could be discovered, tested, and utilized. Nor can we predict what laws will be discovered by generations of scientists sifting data for evidence of the effects of the unseen. It would have been impossible five hundred years ago to predict anything of the laws of thermodynamics or nuclear physics, let alone the devising of experiments to test and establish them as laws. The difficulties of bringing to light, of describing and testing the laws of the spirit, are not any less than those which faced chemists two hundred years ago.

Studying and teaching the laws of the spirit should benefit humanity in even greater measure than did, for example, the laws of chemistry. Matthew Arnold thought that the decreasing influence of the Bible in the nineteenth century could be reversed if the ideals and hopes and laws expressed in the poetic and allegorical language of the scriptures could be explored experimentally. He hoped that dogmatic theology could be succeeded by empirical theology or experimental theology. If people could understand religious principles in their own everyday language rather than in ancient metaphors, they might take them more seriously.

More benefits may result in the domains of the spirit if each individual were to draw up his own personal list of the laws governing spiritual matters. Of course, this would be easier if he first studied the books and articles of scientists engaged in investigating powerful laws of the spirit. However, only when we understand and claim as our own some actual laws of the spirit do we begin to build our own heaven. What could be more uplifting than for each human to write in his mind and heart, as well as on paper, the various laws by which he ought to live? He may measure his spiritual growth if every year he revises and rewrites his own personal list of laws. How beneficial it would be if every school each day devoted a few minutes to help each pupil study the laws of the spirit as they are brought to light and formulated by great scientists, so that each person could improve his own written list. The supreme moments in the life of each of us occur whenever we grasp a new inspiring truth and appropriate it so that it revitalizes our personality and becomes a part of our life.

When any field of research is begun, no one can possibly predict what may be discovered eventually. Astronomers before Copernicus could not have predicted or even imagined galaxies, or supernovas, or pulsars. Even so, no one can yet say what laws of the spirit will be formulated and proven eventually.[1]

Sir John goes on to give some examples of laws of the spirit that might be researched by experimental and statistical methods.

As a person thinks, so is that person. This example is generally agreed upon by all religions. Its benefit, if taught to young people, could be the basis for future generations to become much more disciplined in the control and management of their minds and lives.[2]

It is interesting that Sir John would suggest this law of the spirit first, for discipline is certainly the hallmark of his own life. As a child, growing up in the small town of Winchester, Tennessee, John was given extraordinary opportunity to develop characteristics of discipline, self-reliance, and enterprise. His father, Harvey Templeton, was a successful lawyer and businessman-investor who gave John an early introduction to thrift and planning. At the age of four John was raising beans in a part of his mother's large garden and selling them at the local country store for a handsome profit. At the age of eight he had developed a very profitable venture selling fireworks to his schoolboy chums. No store in Winchester sold fireworks, so John found an outlet in Ohio that supplied them at a good price. At the appropriate time for fireworks—Christmas and the Fourth of July—he would make a good profit and his friends would be happy to provide it!

John's mother also had a great impact on his character. Vella Handly Templeton was a well-educated woman for those days. She had attended grammar school and high school in Winchester, then had gone on to study mathematics, Greek, and Latin for seven years at Winchester Normal College. At the age of thirty she married Harvey Templeton, and they settled into a comfortable home in Winchester. The Templetons were relatively well-to-do and yet followed a pattern of thrift that John has carried on all through his life. John, his mother, and his brother Harvey had charge accounts at all the local stores but charged very little. His requests for money from his father were always granted, and he was given free rein in choosing his activities. Only very rarely did his parents give him any advice on ethics, religion, business, or school. This freedom in choosing, with only gentle parental influence, was a tactic deliberately chosen by the elder Templetons and came largely out of a philosophy of living that stemmed from Vella Templeton's religious convictions. She believed that self-reliance depended on making decisions for oneself, rather than letting others do the deciding. An active member of the Cumberland Presbyterian Church, she also had a deep commitment to another religious group, the fledgling Unity School of Christianity. From this source John learned some key lessons for his future. One of these was that happiness and success result from "thought control," concentrating one's mind on positive and productive things. Material success and wealth, said Unity founder Charles Fillmore, flow naturally from spiritual growth and progress.

That happiness stems from spiritual growth also follows from these ideas, and this is another of Sir John's suggested laws of the spirit, a law he seems to aptly substantiate, and which he feels should be researched and documented. This is a lesson he has learned well. William Proctor, in his book *The Templeton Prizes*, makes the point that John Templeton has used his wealth to fulfill deeply held values, and this is the real secret of his happiness.

> But there is also another important side to the highest levels of happiness and success in investing—a side that encompasses far broader considerations than just the "nuts and bolts" techniques of accumulating wealth. As we'll see, it's essential to understand and affirm this broader dimension of making big money if you want to be *truly* successful and live happily with your wealth once you acquire it. Too often a person may forge ahead and do quite well in building up his personal assets. But then the unexpected pressures and temptations of his newfound wealth present so many problems that his "success" turns out to be not a success at all, but rather a curse in disguise.
>
> But Templeton has learned how to be comfortable with his riches. He's a self-made man who didn't have the benefit of a family tradition of "old money" and philanthropy, but he has avoided the danger of being "blown away" by his wealth because he has learned the secret of "successful living with success." Indeed, John Templeton provides one of the best living examples of how a person's wealth can become a satisfying extension of his inner drives and values.[3]

In addition to these two laws Sir John would add two laws about giving. In the first he talks about love:

> The more love we give away, the more we have left. The laws of love differ from the laws of arithmetic. Love hoarded dwindles, but love given grows. If we give all our love, we will have more left than he who saves some. Giving love, not receiving, is important; but when we give with no thought of receiving, we automatically and inescapably receive abundantly. Heaven is a by-product of love. When we say "I love you," we mean that "a little of God's love flows from us to you." But, thereby, we do not love less, but more. For in flowing the quantity is magnified. God's love is infinite, and is directed equally to

each person, but it seems to gain intensity when directed to sinners. This is the wonder and mystery of it, that when we love God we get an enormous increase in the quantity flowing through us to others.[4]

To further validate this law, Sir John quotes from the first epistle of John, the appeal to the early church to love one another as the proof of their new relationship to God, and then concludes with a superlative quotation from St. Paul's first epistle to the Corinthians:

> And now I will show you the best way of all. I may speak in tongues of men or of angels, but if I am without love, I am a sounding gong or a clanging cymbal. I may have the gift of prophecy, and know every hidden truth; I may have faith strong enough to move mountains; but if I have no love, I am nothing. I may dole out all I possess, or even give my body to be burnt, but if I have no love, I am none the better.
>
> Love is patient; love is kind and envies no one. Love is never boastful, nor conceited, nor rude; never selfish, not quick to take offence. Love keeps no score of wrongs; does not gloat over other men's sins, but delights in the truth. There is nothing love cannot face; there is no limit to its faith, its hope, and its endurance.
>
> Love will never come to an end. Are there prophets? Their work will be over. Are there tongues of ecstasy? They will cease. Is there knowledge? It will vanish away; for our knowledge and our prophecy alike are partial, and the partial vanishes when wholeness comes. When I was a child, my speech, my outlook, and my thoughts were all childish. When I grew up, I had finished with childish things. Now we see only puzzling reflections in a mirror, but then we shall see face to face. My knowledge now is partial; then it will be whole, like God's knowledge of me. In a word, there are three things that last for ever: faith, hope, and love; but the greatest of them all is love (1 Cor. 12:31–13:13, NEB).[5]

The second law about giving is a very familiar one. Sir John says:

It is better to give than to receive. Giving is a sign of psychological and spiritual maturity. There are few diseases so childish and so deadly as the "gimmies," a disease that separates us from friends and from God, and shrinks the soul. The secret of success is giving, not getting. To get joy we must give it and to keep joy we must scatter it. The greatest charity is to help a person change from being a receiver to being a giver.[6]

Being only a receiver does indeed separate us from our friends and from God, and the resultant loneliness of body and spirit is the basis for another suggestion for a law of the spirit:

Loneliness is the punishment for those who want to get, not give. Helping others is the cure for loneliness. If we feel lonely, we are probably self-centered. If we feel unloved, we are probably unloving. If we love only ourselves, we may be the only persons to love us. Whatever we give out, we get back.[7]

Along with the truth that self-centeredness leads to loneliness, Sir John adds a law about the nature of forgiveness.

To be forgiven, we must first forgive. Forgiving brings forgiveness. Failure to forgive creates a hell for the unforgiver, not the unforgiven.[8]

Psychologists tell us that healing from a hurt someone has done to you must begin with your forgiveness of that person. I recall once mentioning to Sir John that a magazine article about him by a former employee was unfair and untrue and that he should write a letter setting the record straight. His response was, "I did write him a letter, but it was to wish him well in his new job and to tell him I was praying for him!"

Then, of course, in this list of candidates for laws of the spirit, Sir John included a law about thanksgiving.

Thanksgiving opens the door to spiritual growth. If there is any day in our life which is not thanksgiving day, then we are not fully alive. Counting our blessings attracts blessings. Counting our blessings each morning starts a day full of blessings. Thanksgiving brings God's bounty. From gratitude comes riches—from complaints poverty. Thankfulness opens the door to happiness. Thanksgiving causes giving. Thanksgiving puts our mind in tune with the Infinite. Continual gratitude dissolves our worries.[9]

Recall that Sir John, in his Templeton College lecture quoted in the Introduction, said that the attitude of thanksgiving had the potential for revolutionizing your life. It is a powerful tool for good, one that he uses continually, and one that his good friend Norman Vincent Peale stressed repeatedly from the pulpit of Marble Collegiate Church in New York City and through *Guideposts* magazine. In 1992, Sir John was awarded the Norman Vincent Peale Award for Positive Thinking.

We should not miss the connection between thanksgiving and giving, for as John says "Thanksgiving *causes* giving." When you are overwhelmed by the thought that God is making his infinite knowledge and love available to you then you want to share it with others. In a letter to Father Robert Sirico of the Acton Institute, Sir John explains his view of thanksgiving and its relationship to giving.

> Humility is especially rewarding when it is humility toward God. When you humbly admit that no human has ever known more than a tiny bit of the infinity and eternity of God, then you desire and seek to learn more. When you humbly admit that God is making available to you his infinite knowledge and love then you want to become a clear and open channel to radiate this knowledge and love to others. Love shrinks when hoarded but multiplies when given away.
>
> People who are overwhelmingly grateful every day for their multitudes of blessings feel a desire to help others. When you are diligently trying to help others not only by producing goods and services but also by radiating love and knowledge then without any intention on your part, others will be attracted to you and you too will grow in prosperity and happiness.[10]

Becoming a channel of blessing to others brings prosperity and happiness to ourselves, he says. Then he adds another related law of the spirit, perhaps the most paradoxical of all:

> Surrender to God brings freedom. It is in dying to our selfish selves (self-denial) that we are born to eternal life.[11]

This law makes sense only if one has put his trust totally in God. In *The Humble Approach* Sir John quotes from Jesus with these words:

> When Jesus was asked what is the greatest law, He said: "Thou shalt love the Lord thy God with all thy heart, and with all thy soul, and with all thy mind. This is the first and great commandment. And second is like unto it, Thou shalt love thy neighbour as thyself. On these two commandments hang all the law and the prophets" (Matt. 22: 37–40, KJB).
>
> This can be researched as a basic law of the spirit. A person who applies this law finds his life revolutionized. Opening our heart to God allows His love to flow through us like a mighty river. If we love God totally as He loves us, we will love each of His children without exception as Jesus Himself described (Luke 6:27–36, KJB). The happiest people on earth are those who love God totally.[12]

Here then are ten laws of the spirit, which are prime candidates for a program of research on spiritual information. To these many more possible laws will be added. In fact, Sir John has expanded the list to two hundred, and published them in 1994 in the form of a book titled *Discovering the Laws of Life* and a revised edition called *Worldwide Laws of Life*.

Discovering the "Laws of Life"

The initial impetus for the assembling of the expanded list of the "Laws of Life" comes from Sir John's desire to build a component of moral and spiritual development into the curriculum of the world's schools. As a boy, he had the experience of seeing the "Laws of Life" in action in a Tennessee school. In April of 1989 he wrote in *Plus,* a publication of the Foundation for Christian Living, founded by Dr. and Mrs. Norman Vincent Peale, about this special school.

> I recall the Webb School, near where I grew up in Winchester, Tenn. That school tried to teach more than reading, writing, and arithmetic. The school was started by an elderly man named Shaunee Webb. The motto of the school was "We Teach Character." Webb regarded it as his principal purpose to teach students the "Laws of Life" along with Latin, history, and mathematics. Many graduates of the Webb School became nationally known, their success based on what they learned from the founder.[13]

Not surprisingly, Sir John's effort to bring a moral development emphasis into the schools was also begun in Sir John's home county, Franklin County, Tennessee. In the Introduction to *Discovering the Laws of Life,* he talks of his hopes for the book and gives a little history of the essay program he began in Franklin County.

> Following in the footsteps of Benjamin Franklin and others who have tried to pass on their learning to others, this book has been written from a lifetime of experience and diligent observation in the hope that it may help people in all parts of the world to make their lives not only happier but also more useful. It is intended for everyone, for the young who each day are being introduced to the laws that can make their lives more productive, as well as for the older and more experienced who seek confirmation and affirmation of the "Laws of Life."
> . . . In this book, you will find two hundred major ones, culled from a list of many hundreds. They come from a vast array of sources—from the Scriptures, from storytellers such as Aesop, from scientists such as Isaac Newton, from artists and historians. The poet Henry Wadsworth Longfellow wrote: "Lives of great men oft remind us that we can make our lives sublime and departing leave behind us footprints in the sands of time." The truth of this statement can be demonstrated if we look to the lives of the famous as well as the unsung heroes of

the past and present, for there we will find many models for useful, happy living. And, when we examine their words and deeds, we will discover the principles that inspired and sustained their benefits to future generations.

. . . Drawn from the scriptures of different traditions, as well as from schools of philosophical thought both ancient and modern, each quotation points to a particular law that holds true for most people under most circumstances. The essays are designed to inspire and encourage you—to help you consider more deeply the laws you live by and to reap the rewards of their practical application. The laws described here are like tools. When you apply them consistently, they have the power to transform your life into a more deeply useful and joyful experience. Even if your life is already working well, it's possible that it will work even better as you incorporate the wisdom contained in these pages. If I had found a book of two hundred basic laws of life during my college years, I could have been far more productive then and in the years that have followed.

A few years ago, I began offering support for a "Laws of Life" essay contest in my boyhood home, Franklin County, Tennessee. Mr. and Mrs. Handly Templeton help in running the program. Prizes for the essays—they run from one hundred to two thousand words in length—are awarded semiannually, with a first prize of $2,000, a second prize of $800, and a number of runner-up prizes. The response has been gratifying. The number of entrants for each six-month period has risen to its present size of six hundred students. It would give me a great pleasure to learn that your hometown wants to embark on its own version of the Franklin County program.

In my teenage years, I was inspired by the courage and vision of Rudyard Kipling's poem "If." This poem taught me to dream—but also to be master of my dreams. I learned from the great English poet that the earth belongs to us all and that, with courage and enthusiasm, progress is likely to follow. The final stanza of "If" still rings in my ears:

If you can fill the unforgiving minutes
With sixty seconds' worth of distance run,
Yours is the Earth and everything that's in it,
And—which is more—you'll be a Man, my son!

Behind this book is my belief that the basic principles for leading a "sublime life," to paraphrase Longfellow, can be examined and tested just as science examines and tests natural laws of the universe. I have a vision that by learning the laws of life and applying them to everyday situations, more and more people will find themselves leading joyous and useful lives.[14]

A later chapter of this book will describe in more detail John Templeton's program for extending the "Laws of Life" program to high schools and colleges in the United States, the United Kingdom, and most recently in Russia. In connection with the John Templeton Foundation's program of research on spiritual laws, the "Laws of Life" will be included with the goal of establishing the most useful and universally acceptable laws for promulgation through the schools and through further frequently improved editions of the book. Sir John emphasizes that the first edition is only a beginning of the search for experimentally verifiable laws of a spiritual nature that are universally accepted and free of sectarian bias. The program of experimental verification will probably focus on statistical methodologies, just as the demonstration of the close relation between cigarette smoking, lung cancer, and heart disease had a statistical, epidemiological basis of verification.

CHAPTER 3

Research in the Sciences

Sir John hopes that rapid progress in obtaining spiritual information ushers in a new renaissance for humanity, and that humility theology science may be a key to success. Intrinsic to Sir John's spiritual investment plan is a multi-faceted research program, emphasizing rigorous scientific methodology and interdisciplinary thinking and characterized by a willingness to take calculated risks in uncertain territory. This strategy is not unusual for John Templeton. In the business world it has made him one of the most successful investment counselors of all time. But now, in place of exhaustive evaluation of a company's future business prospects, Sir John thoughtfully examines the accelerating discoveries in the sciences, which point so clearly to deeper Reality. And in similarity to the unbiased, worldwide diversity of his Templeton Growth Fund, he now emphasizes the essential nature of theology-science interaction where each side is listening to and learning from the other. And finally, the calculated risk, which is always a part of profitable investing, but one that can be greatly minimized by diversity and by careful research, must in this new context be undertaken with daring and courage if the old entrenched ideas of traditional religion and sometimes dogmatic science are to be improved.

Research at the Limits of Science

Of course, we have already discussed in Chapter 1 some of the scientific discoveries that suggest that the visible and tangible may be only a tiny part of the underlying spiritual Reality. Sir John plans to encourage scientific research of this type, to seek further evidence of the work and purpose of the fundamental, creative, spiritual Reality through astronomy, physics, biology, and other hard sciences. He has already edited one book, *Evidence of Purpose*, with chapters by some of the outstanding scientists of the twentieth century, including Owen Gingerich, professor of astronomy and of the history of science at Harvard University and a senior astronomer at the Smithsonian Astrophysical Observatory; Sir John Polkinghorne, Fellow of the Royal Society and former chair of mathematical physics at Cambridge University, who is also an Anglican priest and just now retiring president of Queens' College, Cambridge; and Sir John Eccles, also a Fellow of the Royal Society and the recipient of the 1963 Nobel Prize for physiology and medicine. Topics covered by these and the other seven contributors include new intimations from science that such ideas as design and purpose are very relevant to our understanding of the cosmos. Professor Paul Davies, a physicist at the University of Adelaide, contributes a chapter on the "Unreasonable Effectiveness of Science," pointing out the remarkable way in which the universe provides understandable answers to our queries. In other words, why should an incredibly complicated universe be governed by laws that can be described in terms of our mathematics? Then too, these laws prove to be special in a number of ways: by their coherence and harmony, their economy, and their universality and dependability. Yet, surprisingly, these same laws allow for a wide range of diversity and complexity instead of leading to total chaos.

In his introduction to *Evidence of Purpose*, Sir John writes:

> This book was written to bring a new scientific perspective to the age-old question of purpose. It had been assumed since

perhaps the middle of the last century that science had put to rest any idea that there was a Creator whose design had brought the universe its form and process. Yet there have been powerful dissenting voices even among the great scientists. Physicists like Albert Einstein openly and movingly spoke of the religious attitude as essential to good science and Sir James Jeans said that the universe was beginning to look not like a great machine but rather like a great thought. Astronomer Allen Sandage spoke of God in terms of the marvelous laws of nature, and Sir Arthur Eddington once wrote of a spiritual world that lies behind the universe we study.

But in the last twenty or thirty years the number of scientists raising philosophical and religious questions as a result of recent scientific discoveries has multiplied. This volume contains some of those questions—searching, exploratory, tentative but often profound—about ultimate reality and purpose and meaning. The scientists who have contributed to this book covered a broad spectrum of theological and philosophical persuasion. Yet they all express something of the wonder of the universe we begin to know through science, and all see evidence for a deep meaning written into the laws and processes of nature.

It is to be hoped that the reader will come to this collection of essays with the same spirit of humility that characterizes all good science. As we begin to understand our own limitations as finite creatures in a vast universe of infinite complexity and intricacy, perhaps we can be released from our prejudices— whether scientific, philosophical, or religious—and open our minds to the great plan of which we are a part.

Science in the past few decades has revolutionized our view of the universe and our place in it. Just a century ago science appeared to be tidying up our world, dispelling the illusions of gods and inexplicable miracles and finally providing us with an "objective" view. Yet today the credo of objectivity, together with its tight little mechanisms and clockwork images, is gone. Matter has lost its tangibility, space and time are no longer separable entities, and quantum physics has shown our world to be more like a symphony of wave forms in dynamic flux than some sort of mechanical contrivance.

Anthropologist Loren Eiseley talks about the illusions of science in his book, *The Firmament of Time.*

> A scientist writing around the turn of the century remarked that all of the past generations of men have lived and died in a world of illusions. The unconscious irony in his observation consists in the fact that this man assumed the progress of science to have been so great that a clear vision of the world without illusion was, by his own time, possible. It is needless to add that he wrote before Einstein, . . . at a time when Mendel was just about to be rediscovered, and before the advances in the study of radioactivity had made their impact—of both illumination and confusion—upon this century.
>
> Certainly science has moved forward. But when science progresses, it often opens vaster mysteries to our gaze. Moreover, science frequently discovers that it must abandon or modify what it once believed. Sometimes it ends by accepting what it has previously scorned. The simplistic idea that science marches undeviatingly down an ever broadening highway can scarcely be sustained by the historian of ideas.

Scientific progress is always attended by the corrections of error, by sharp shifts in direction and emphasis. And the nature of the correction is again only tentative, only partially truth. And the illusions could hardly be said to have been dispelled. In fact, in a very real sense, what we have started with as the tangible—matter, energy, space, and time—now seems to bear some of the mystery of an illusion. Things are not what they seemed. In the words of science writer K. C. Cole:

> So much of science consists of things we can never see: light "waves" and charged "particles;" magnetic "fields" and gravitational "forces;" quantum "jumps" and electron "orbits." In fact, none of these phenomena is literally what we say it is. Light waves do not undulate through empty space in the same way that water waves ripple over a still pond; a field is only a mathematical description of the strength and direction of a force; an atom does not literally jump from

one quantum state to another; and electrons do not really travel around the atomic nucleus in orbits. The words we use are merely metaphors. "When it comes to atoms," wrote Neils Bohr, "language can be used only as in poetry. The poet, too, is not merely so concerned with describing facts as with creating images."[1]

The most astounding thing about our recent discoveries in the sciences is that each answer seems not only to raise many more questions, but that the questions now seem to extend far beyond the capacities of ordinary previous experimentation to provide answers. If the answers sought before were only partial, the questions raised now are difficult to frame as scientific questions; perhaps we are peering into a whole new dimension, a new Reality. Paul Davies deals with this phenomenon in the final chapter of his book *The Mind of God*, describing the frustration of some of his colleagues and the effort to avoid the whole issue on the part of many others. He concludes with some important thoughts about mysticism:

> Most scientists have a deep mistrust of mysticism. This is not surprising, as mystical thought lies at the opposite extreme to rational thought, which is the basis of the scientific method. Also, mysticism tends to be confused with the occult, the paranormal, and other fringe beliefs. In fact, many of the world's finest thinkers, including some notable scientists such as Einstein, Pauli, Schrödinger, Heisenberg, Eddington, and Jeans, have also espoused mysticism. My own feeling is that the scientific method should be pursued as far as it possibly can. Mysticism is no substitute for scientific inquiry and logical reasoning so long as this approach can be consistently applied. It is only in dealing with ultimate questions that science and logic may fail us. I am not saying that science and logic are likely to provide the wrong answers, but they may be incapable of addressing the sort of "why" (as opposed to "how") questions we want to ask.
>
> The expression "mystical experience" is often used by religious people, or those who practice meditation. These

experiences, which are undoubtedly real enough for the person who experiences them, are said to be hard to convey in words. Mystics frequently speak of an overwhelming sense of being at one with the universe or with God, of glimpsing a holistic vision of reality, or of being in the presence of a powerful and loving influence. Most important, mystics claim that they can grasp *ultimate reality* in a single experience, in contrast to the long and tortuous deductive sequence (petering out in turtle trouble) of the logical-scientific method of inquiry. Sometimes the mystical path seems to involve little more than an inner sense of peace—"a compassionate, joyful stillness that lies beyond the activity of busy minds" was the way a physicist colleague once described it to me. Einstein spoke of a "cosmic religious feeling" that inspired his reflections on the order and harmony of nature. Some scientists, most notably the physicists Brian Josephson and David Bohm, believe that regular mystical insights achieved by quiet meditative practices can be a useful guide in the formulation of scientific theories.[2]

Sir John believes these mystical experiences are just what one would expect from the Creator God who is bringing His plan for accelerating growth in spiritual knowledge to fruition. Research into these meditative insights, as well as a deeper probing of purpose and meaning in the universe, will be a major effort of the Templeton Foundation and hopefully many others who will join the search in the years ahead. The benefits in terms of our deeper understanding of ourselves and our purpose in the cosmos could be immense.

Research on Purpose in the Universe

Another closely related human attribute with great benefit for study is purpose, the experience all of us share in our immediate planning for short-term goals and in our long-term dreaming of what could be. What is the source of this characteristic, if it is not a mark in miniature of the Creator in his creature? We should know much more about purpose, and especially re-examine our studies of other living organisms that seem to display purpose.

In his chapter in *Evidence of Purpose,* David Wilcox writes about the stubborn refusal of biologists to allow any teleological (purposive) explanations into their science—"teleophobia," he calls it. Such bias, he says, has hampered important studies of probable built-in restraints in the evolutionary process and narrowed developments in this area of our understanding, especially as they might provide evidence for design.[3] This is probably only one of a number of areas of science in which empirical studies may be hampered by a selection against research, which might provide data for purpose in the universe, just as scientists resisted the Big Bang theory for the origin of the universe because of its probable theological significance. An emphasis upon freely conceived research, open to whatever direction the data takes, would be of great benefit to our understanding of our evolutionary past and in planning for a viable future for the human race. Further evidence for design in the evolutionary process would provide a temporizing and humbling influence on those scientists who are resistant to theistic arguments. It would also greatly challenge some members of the theological community who still shun scientific data as irrelevant or dangerous.

Research on Human Creativity

John Templeton is also keenly interested in human creativity, in part because of its implication that we are the products of an incredibly creative process, which had us in mind, and in part because we may have been hampered in our creative development because of an unwillingness to fully explore human creative potential through empirical and statistical research methods. Neural science research is now showing that we use only perhaps 10 percent of our available brain cells at any one time. This strongly suggests that human brain function could be greatly enhanced if proper conditions could be found for mobilizing the remaining neural networks. This suggestion is also supported by limited data on so-called idiot savants, who show remarkable abilities in mathematics or in music, although their general abilities are quite limited. What is implied here is that the human brain can perform incredible functions under certain conditions. Finding these conditions for individuals with general mental abilities could be a tremendous potential benefit to the mental development of human beings. Beyond this lies the distinct possibility that research may demonstrate that spiritual attributes might also be greatly enhanced under certain conditions, thus leading to a greatly accelerated spiritual development of humankind.

In this connection, Paul Davies relates in *The Mind of God* what he calls mystical experiences, which have happened to scientists in the course of their scientific theorizing. Davies mentions physicist Roger Penrose's description of his experience of mathematical inspirations as a sudden "breaking through" into a Platonic realm, and he also shares a report that mathematician Kurt Gödel spoke of "other relation to reality" by which he could directly perceive mathematical objects, like infinity, by meditative means. Perhaps his most interesting story is that of the famous cosmologist Fred Hoyle, who experienced what Davies calls "a truly religious (as opposed to merely Platonic) event" while driving through the north of England, on his way to a vacation in the Scottish Highlands in the late 1960s. According to Davies, Hoyle had been working at Cambridge with his collaborator Jayant Narlikar on a cosmological theory of electromagnetism that involved some very challenging mathematics, and decided to take a break to go hiking with some colleagues. The story of his experience was later written in a report published by the University of Cardiff. Hoyle writes:

> As the miles slipped by I turned the quantum mechanical problem . . . over in my mind, in the hazy way I normally have in thinking mathematics in my head. Normally, I have to write things down on paper, and then fiddle with the equations and

integrals as best I can. But somewhere on Bowes Moor my awareness of the mathematics clarified, not a little, not even a lot, but as if a huge brilliant light had suddenly been switched on. How long did it take to become totally convinced that the problem was solved? Less than five seconds. It only remained to make sure that before the clarity faded I had enough of the essential steps stored safely in my recallable memory. It is indicative of the measure of certainty I felt that in the ensuing days I didn't trouble to commit anything to paper. When ten days or so later I returned to Cambridge I found it possible to write out the thing without difficulty.[4]

Paul Davies analyzes Hoyle's experience as follows:

Hoyle believes that the organization of the cosmos is controlled by a "superintelligence" who guides its evolution through quantum processes. . . . Furthermore, Hoyle's is a teleological God (somewhat like that of Aristotle or Teilhard de Chardin) directing the world toward a final state in the infinite future. Hoyle believes that by acting at the quantum level this superintelligence can implant thoughts or ideas from the future, ready-made, into the human brain. This, he suggests, is the origin of both mathematical and musical inspiration.[5]

Others, too, have experienced these moments of clarity and insight. Davies says that Hoyle was told by the Nobel prize-winning physicist Richard Feynman that several times he had experienced moments of inspiration, which were followed in each case by an intense feeling of euphoria lasting two or three days.

These are important data for the Templeton research program, because they strongly suggest that great resources of mind may be accessible if the conditions are examined carefully and systematically. Paul Davies is very impressed with the existence of mind in the universe. He concludes his book with these searching words:

The central theme that I have explored in this book is that, through science, we human beings are able to grasp at least some of nature's secrets. We have cracked part of the cosmic code. Why this should be, just why *Homo sapiens* should carry the spark of rationality that provides the key to the universe, is a deep enigma. We who are children of the universe—animated stardust—can nevertheless reflect on the nature of that same universe, even to the extent of glimpsing the rules on which it runs. How we have become linked into this cosmic dimension is a mystery. Yet the linkage cannot be denied.

What does it mean? What is Man that we might be party to such privilege? I cannot believe that our existence in this universe is a mere quirk of fate, an accident of history, an incidental blip in the great cosmic drama. Our involvement is too intimate. The physical species *Homo* may count for nothing, but the existence of mind in some organism on some planet in the universe is surely a fact of fundamental significance. Through conscious beings the universe has generated self-awareness. This can be no trivial detail, no minor byproduct of mindless, purposeless forces. We are truly meant to be here. [6]

Of course, what Davies refers to here as mind would have much of the character that John Templeton would define as spirit. The experiences of penetrating insight, of sudden appearance of solutions to seemingly intractable scientific problems, the euphoria that follows, the incredible creativity that musical and mathematical inspiration often entails, the sense of the presence of an awesome force (mentioned as the experience of physicist Russell Stannard, for one, in his book *Grounds for Reasonable Belief* [7]), the "cosmic religious feeling" of Albert Einstein, all are essentially spiritual experiences and seem most often to be so viewed by those who experience them. How can these spiritual experiences, which are so valuable to the individuals involved, be extended to a much wider fraction of society?

CHAPTER 4

Research on the Role of Spirituality in Medicine

Sir John Templeton's desire to encourage progress in spiritual information through science also includes the expectation that medicine's great advances in treating physical illness can find complementary expression in the spiritual realm. Indeed, a strong move is currently under way in America to diversify medical treatment approaches to include a variety of previously excluded therapies, including spiritual ones. In addition, the John Templeton Foundation has given strong support to studies conducted by Dr. David Larson, director of the National Institute for Healthcare Research (NIHR). These studies demonstrate that religious variables are neglected in clinical research and in the practice of medicine. In most cases these variables demonstrate a strong positive relationship between spirituality and health.

Is Religion the Forgotten Factor in Medicine?

In a lecture sponsored by the John Templeton Foundation for presentation at medical schools, Dr. Dale Matthews of Georgetown University School of Medicine explains that a wall of separation has gradually come between medicine and religion. Yet it was not always this way. Medicine and religion had worked hand in hand for thousands of years. Illness was perceived in ancient societies as primarily a spiritual problem and religious and medical authority was vested in the same person (e.g., an Aaronic priest) who might himself become an object of worship (e.g., Imhotep, Ascalupius, Jesus Christ). This close relationship between medicine and religion remained until the seventeenth century when empirical science challenged church authority with the eventual result that the religions generally relinquished concern for the physical body (and later still, the mind), leaving the soul as the church's domain. As Ian Barbour points out in his *Religion in an Age of Science*, by the twentieth century religion and medical science were perceived as mutually exclusive and inharmonious; while science was portrayed as factual, empirically verifiable, and objective, religion was seen as ephemeral, subjective, and ambiguous. Indeed, the National Academy of Science, in its 1984 resolution concerning the teaching about origins, declared that "religion and science are mutually exclusive realms of human thought whose presentation in the same context leads to misunderstanding of both scientific theory and religious belief."

Contrasting Religious Attitudes of Patients and Health-Care Providers

But near the end of the twentieth century, change is again under way and a new rapprochement between medicine and religion is a distinct possibility. The reasons for this development lie for the most part at the doorstep of the medical scientific establishment, which is experiencing a loss of confidence and sensing a growing disillusionment among the larger society. According to the National Institute for Healthcare Research, surveys indicate that the American people are highly religious; 95 percent believe in God, 80 percent believe the Bible is the actual or inspired Word of God, 72 percent agree that "my whole approach to life is based on my religion," 57 percent pray at least once a day, 46 percent describe themselves as having been "born again," and 42 percent attend worship services once a week. Furthermore, a significant number of Americans participate in religious healing activities. A 1986 survey of 586 adults in Richmond, Virginia, indicated that 14 percent reported physical healings such as recovery from viral infections, cancers, back problems, emotional problems, and fractures by means of prayer or divine intervention. And in another survey of 325 adults, 30 percent reported praying regularly for healing and for health maintenance. Additional research data can be obtained through the National Institute for Healthcare Research, 6110 Executive Blvd., Suite 908 Rockville, MD, 10852.

In contrast to these observations, the surveys indicate that health professionals are significantly less religious than the general public. One study reported that 33 percent of psychologists, 39 percent of psychiatrists, 46 percent of social workers, and 62 percent of marriage and family therapists agree that "my whole approach to life is based on my religion" compared to 72 percent of the American public. Similar results have been found for 146 family physicians in Vermont in a 1991 study. The irony in these situations is, of course, that while most patients expect religious values to be addressed by their doctor, the average physician is not prepared to address the real contribution spirituality may bring to the healing process.

Attitudes of Medical Scientists

Now, if we shift from medical practice to medical research, the same kind of neglect of religious variables has been found by Dr. David Larson in an in-depth study of the clinical literature by a process he calls systematic view. One example of this work, titled "Systematic Analysis of Research on Religious Variables in Four Major Psychiatric Journals, 1978–1982," was published in the *American Journal of Psychiatry* in 1986. In this article, 2,348 psychiatric studies published over a five-year period were examined for religious variables. It was found that only 2.5 percent of the studies used a religious measure (e.g., denomination) while only 0.1 percent used religion as a central variable, and only one study used a validated, multi-dimensional measure of religious commitment. Seventy-two percent of these studies showed a positive effect for religious commitment.

The great value of Larson's approach to review lies in its more rigorous methodology, in which strict quantitative research methods are used to arrive at more objective results. This has been especially important in the case of social policy literature reviews, which previously had been done in a much less systematic manner with frequently biased results. This approach, analyzing the clinical research work already published, has been of great interest to Sir John Templeton, and he has provided significant support for Dr. David Larson and the NIHR. Funds have been provided by the John Templeton Foundation for a compilation of the most current research conducted on spirituality and health. More than four hundred abstracts of published research articles have been published in the past three years in three volumes with the title, *The Faith Factor: An Annotated Bibliography of Clinical Research on Spiritual Subjects.* Dr. Dale Matthews has been a co-author with Dr. Larson of this series. A fourth volume is in preparation. The chosen articles focused primarily on three areas of particular interest to Sir John: love or altruism, prayer, and well-being. This research has also given strong support to the thesis that religious variables are neglected in clinical research and that there can be major benefits of religious commitment in terms of health care. In terms of overall benefits, consider the following:

> Of 212 studies examining the effects of religious commitment on health care outcomes, 160 (75%) demonstrated a positive benefit of religious commitment while 37 (17%) revealed a mixed effect or no effect, and 15 (7%) demonstrated a negative effect.

The positive benefits of religious commitment for psychiatric illness were even more striking. Dr. Matthews cites the results of the review as follows:

> Positive effects of religious commitment were found in 15 of 15 (100%) of studies of drug abuse, 18 of 19 (95%) of studies of adjustment and coping, 20 of 24 (83%) of studies of alcohol abuse, 15 of 18 (83%) of psychopathology studies, and 13 of 19 (68%) of studies of depression.

The foregoing suggests strongly to Sir John that a major research effort should be mounted to study the effect of prayer and other spiritual interventions under the most rigorous empirical scientific conditions with diverse populations and religions. Certainly this area of study holds great promise in re-establishing the place of religion in the healing process.

Also of great importance is the changing of attitudes among medical scientists and clinicians. Already there are signs of change in the federal bureaucracy, with the establishment of the Office of Alternative Medicine within the National Institutes of Health, and the advent of a new journal, *Alternative Therapies in Health and Medicine,* edited by Dr. Larry Dossey, another close associate of Sir John. In his editorial in the first issue, titled "A Journal and a Journey," Dossey recalled some of the salient examples of scientists' intransigence in the face of new data and new ideas.

> History is also replete with examples of how scientists themselves can be part of the problem, just like anyone else. Marcello Truzzi, professor of sociology at Eastern Michigan University in Ypsilanti, Michigan, and director of the Center for Scientific Anomalies Research in Ann Arbor, Michigan, has said, "Many studies in the psychology of science . . . indicate that scientists are at least as dogmatic and authoritarian, at least as foolish and illogical as everybody else, including when they do science." Truzzi enumerates many examples from the history of science in which narrowness eclipsed open-mindedness. Lord Kelvin pronounced that X-rays would be a hoax. Thomas Watson, once chairman of the board of IBM, declared

in 1943, "I think there is a world market for about five computers." In 1889 Charles Duell, commissioner of the U.S. Office of Patents, penned a letter to President McKinley asking him to abolish the patents office since "everything that can be invented has been invented." Ernst Mach, the physicist whose ideas influenced the young Einstein, said he could not accept the theory of relativity any more than he could accept the existence of atoms. Thomas Edison, reports Truzzi, said that he saw no commercial use for the light bulb. When the French Academy of Science invited a demonstration of the phonograph, one scientist leaped from his chair, seized the exhibitor, began shaking him, and shouted, "I won't be taken in by your ventriloquist!" Lord Rutherford declared atomic power "moonshine." And so on.

The history of medicine includes numerous instances in which physicians have rejected new ideas, even in the face of compelling data. A dramatic example took place in the nineteenth century on the obstetric wards of Allgemeines Krankenhaus, a famous hospital in Vienna. The struggle involved a technique that was heretical for the time: handwashing. So high was the mortality rate from childbirth fever or puerperal sepsis at this hospital that women giving birth begged in tears not to be taken there.

One of the physicians, Ignaz Phillipp Semmelweis (1818–65), noticed that the first obstetric ward was different from the second, which had a lower mortality rate in that students came into the first ward directly from the cadaver dissecting room with unclean hands, and made vaginal examinations of the pregnant women without washing. The second ward, in contrast, was devoted to the instruction of midwives, who devoted much greater attention to hygiene and personal cleanliness. Noting these differences, Semmelweis theorized that the students were spreading the disease. He immediately instituted hygienic precautions: simply washing the hands in a solution of calcium chloride while dealing with pregnant women in labor. As a result, the fatality rate in labor cases fell the first year from 9.92 percent to 3.8 percent and in the following year, to 1.27 percent.

In spite of the data, Semmelweis met with fierce opposition. He was persecuted by many of the leading medical figures of the day. Essentially hounded out of Vienna, he went to the University of Budapest where in 1861 he published his immortal treatise on "The Cause, Concept, and Prophylaxis of Puerperal Fever," as well as his scathing "Open Letters to Sundry Professors of Obstetrics." The result proved devastating for Semmelweis: the strain of controversy brought on insanity and suicide. In spite of this sordid chapter in the history of unconventional medical practices, his contribution today speaks for itself. "He is one of medicine's martyrs," medical historian F. H. Garrison stated, "and in the future, will be one of its far-shining names, for every child-bearing woman owes something to him."

Pharisaical, dogmatic objections often echo in the most hallowed halls of academic medicine, as when the handwashing debate erupted in a firestorm of controversy in Boston at the Harvard Medical School and in nearby Philadelphia. Here the central figure was Oliver Wendell Holmes, who was Parkman professor of anatomy. In February 1843 Holmes read a paper, "On the Contagiousness of Puerperal Fever," in which he affirmed that (1) women "in childbed" should never be attended by physicians who have been conducting autopsies or dealing with cases of puerperal fever; (2) the disease may be conveyed in this fashion from patient to patient; and (3) washing one's hands in calcium chloride and changing one's garments after attending a case of puerperal fever might prevent the disease from spreading. He was attacked by some of the greatest obstetricians of his time. Like Semmelweis, Holmes persisted. In 1855 he delivered his monograph, "Puerperal Fever as a Private Pestilence," reiterating his stance and citing Semmelweis's scientific findings which, as in Vienna, were slow in turning the heads of doubters.

These examples are a reminder that, when it comes to failures of judgment toward unconventional, alternative developments in science, everyone—lay persons and scientists alike—has dirty hands. For scientists, these lapses in clear thinking often take the shape of rejection-without-investigation, as when one scientist, speaking about anomalies in parapsychology research, said, "This is the kind of thing that I would not believe in even if it existed." For lay persons, the error frequently lies in the other direction: uncritical acceptance-without-investigation. For both errors, science can be an antidote. Truzzi again:

> Despite serious questions about how well the system works, I believe in the process of science and scientific progress. Science is a self-correcting system. Encouragement of fair play and due process in the scientific arena will allow that self-correction to work best. A diversity of opinions and dialogue is extremely important. We cannot close the door to maverick claims.

It would be naive to suppose that medicine has ever been, or is likely ever to be, free of contentiousness. Indeed, it would be disastrous if medical science were an exercise in polite agreement. As Arnold Relman, former editor of the New England Journal of Medicine, has said: "Nothing would be further from the truth than to imagine that contemporary medicine is all cut and dried, an accumulated store of tried and tested facts and techniques. The truth is that medicine is, and always has been, in a continual state of ferment and remodeling. It is plagued by ignorance and therefore perpetually agitated by controversy. Controversy has in fact, always been an integral part of medicine, one of its most important and characteristic features. . . . Science and controversy are inseparable companions."

We agree with this point of view. Modern medicine is not fully formed, and we believe researchers in unconventional areas have much to contribute. Indeed, they always have. As Oliver Wendell Holmes observed in 1883 in his Medical Essays (albeit in language that today is considered insensitive):

> It (medicine) learned from a monk how to use antimony, from a Jesuit how to cure agues, from a friar how to cut for stone, from a soldier how to treat gout, from a sailor how to keep off scurvy, from a postmaster how to sound the Eustachian tube, from a dairy-maid how to prevent smallpox,

from an old market-woman how to catch the itch-insect. It borrowed acupuncture and the moxa from the Japanese heathen, and was taught the use of lebelia by the American savage.

Alternative Therapies will enter the ferment that is medical progress, with the hope of contributing to the remodeling that is incessantly occurring in the medical sciences. In so doing, we will not advocate any particular alternative therapies; neither will we be "selling" an exclusive point of view. Our challenge to both the alternative and orthodox medical communities is the same: to honor the tenets of science, to set aside preconceived biases, to follow empirical evidence wherever it may lead.

In so doing, we hope to be guided by Plato's observation in his *Dialogues*. ". . . We are not simply contending in order that my view or that of yours may prevail, but I presume we ought both of us to be fighting for the truth."

Please join us in this fight for the truth—upon which journey this journal now begins.

Sir John Templeton would be quick to point out that humility theology science has as much to offer the medical scientist in terms of a challenge to prideful attitudes as it offers to theologians. We are all learners in God's school!

Changing the Attitudes of Medical Educators

Sir John has also fostered another avenue of investment in changing attitudes, again through the NIHR. This time the focus is on the American medical educational establishment, whose attitudes toward religion are not unlike physicians in practice and medical scientists in clinical research. To create a positive impact on these negative attitudes, Sir John has supported the development of an independent study guide targeted at professionals and graduate students in medicine, social work, psychology, and pastoral counseling. The study guide is composed of seven study modules, which lead participants through published empirical findings on the relationship between spiritual factors and various aspects of physical and mental health. Introductory sections detail the historical neglect of spiritual factors by the health-care profession and also discuss the complexities of measuring variables such as spirituality and religious commitment.

In addition to this module series, there is also the NIHR-directed Faith and Medicine Program, including the lecture program mentioned previously, in which Dr. Dale Matthews is lecturing nationwide at medical schools concerning the beneficial impact that religious commitment can have on physical and mental health as well as discussing the relevance of religious factors in health-care. In order to publicize this program, a mailing containing promotional materials on Dr. Matthews's lectures was sent to all 126 medical schools in the U.S. A survey was also included in the mass mailing to ascertain the state of each medical school's curriculum concerning spirituality, religion, health. Dr. Matthews has received a surprisingly large number of calls in response to these lectures at medical schools nationwide, including John's Hopkins University, Walter Reed Army Medical Center, the University of Maryland, Ohio State University, Vanderbilt Medical School, and the State University of New York Medical Center at Syracuse.

The second component of the Faith and Medicine Program includes a competitive grant program funded by the John Templeton Foundation for the development of a curriculum that integrates religious components with medical care. This competition was advertised and promoted in Dr. Matthews's mass mailing as well as in several medical journals, including the *Journal of the American Medical Association* and the *Journal of General Internal Medicine.* As a result of these promotional activities, NIHR received more than forty inquiries regarding the competition for curriculum development. A panel of judges evaluated each grant application, with five grants of $10,000 each awarded to the winning schools. In the second year the foundation awarded grants to twenty-five more medical schools in America.

A third component of the program is a video exploring the relationship between religion and health. Professionally produced by a public relations company, the video, *Body, Mind, and Spirit,* contains interviews with Dr. Matthews as well as many of the speakers who presented at a recent Templeton Foundation-sponsored conference on "Spiritual Dimensions in Clinical Research."

Finally, NIHR and its staff are developing a model curriculum for psychiatric residents focused on promoting the importance of patient spirituality in psychiatric assessment, treatment, and care. Working in conjunction with a group of nationally recognized psychiatrists interested in encouraging clinical sensitivity to religious issues, NIHR has completed a draft of the pioneering model curriculum and is beginning work on an accompanying study guide. A curriculum such as this is sorely needed as all accredited psychiatric residency programs were mandated to include courses on sensitivity to patient religious issues as of January 1995. This opening to religious issues is encouraging given psychiatry's long-standing antagonism toward the religious sector, and NIHR is hopeful that this model curriculum will help to better educate future psychiatrists as well as encourage a more accepting and open attitude toward religious issues in the clinical setting.

New Research Opportunities

The systematic review approach has proven very fruitful, and Sir John is eager to see it extended to other areas of health care. Given the importance of living longer to clinicians, researchers, and policy makers, NIHR has undertaken a systematic review of the longevity research in order to determine whether the religiously committed actually live longer than the nonreligious. NIHR is collaborating with three of its research fellows, Dr. John Lyons, Dr. Jeffrey Levin, and Dr.

Harold Koenig, in this important effort. Not only will the systematic review reveal whether the religiously committed actually live longer, but it will also explore how frequently and how adequately religious variables are included in the longevity research.

Finally, in the longer term, Sir John is looking for empirical studies of the impact of prayer, meditation, love, thankfulness, and many other characteristics of the spiritual life, all conducted under the most rigorous experimental protocols in a variety of cultural and religious settings. Encouraging the few trained investigators in this field, and providing peer-reviewed journals in which they may publish their findings, are among the highest priority goals of the John Templeton Foundation.

Another key player in this program of growth and recognition is Dr. Herbert Benson, author of the best-selling book, *The Relaxation Response,* and director of the Mind-Body Medical Institute and associate professor of medicine at the Harvard Medical School. Under Dr. Benson's direction, a major course titled "Spirituality and Healing" was convened in Boston in December 1995. It brought together several hundred health professionals to hear about the current data on spiritual variables and health and then to hear a variety of perspectives from representatives of different cultural and religious groups. This three-day course offered continuing medical education credit and may be the beginning of a strong upsurge of interest in spiritual healing in the medical context.

In any case, it is unlikely that Sir John's enthusiasm for medical research into the relationship between the spirit and healing will lessen, nor that the Foundation will be any less enthusiastic in years to come. Sir John's son, Dr. J. M. Templeton, Jr., former professor of pediatric surgery at the University of Pennsylvania Medical School, has become president of the Templeton Foundations. He is likewise deeply concerned for the spiritual dimensions in medicine.

CHAPTER 5

A Call to Humility

Theology Is Often Resistant to New Ideas

 So often scholarship is associated with pride. For many intelligent people, knowing more than others seems to be almost more important than the acquisition of knowledge itself. John Marks Templeton has observed that this tendency of the human ego has been especially destructive of progress in our knowledge of God. Disciples of the founding prophets of the great religions often took an exclusive view of their knowledge of God, and assumed that there was little new to be learned. Research has often been backward-looking, focusing on the ancient foundation instead of the future. In an interview with the publication *Second Opinion* in July 1993, Sir John was asked about his view that none of the great religions seem willing to experiment with openness.

> The main restraining influence has been and is personal ego—the concept that we are the center. For countless ages various people thought that the earth was flat, because it *looks* flat. For countless ages various people have thought that the sun revolved around the earth, because it *looks* that way. For countless ages people have thought that their god was the only true God. The Jews were not the only ones to think they were the chosen people. And the human ego has in effect said that God

is understandable. Human ego has led most religions—I'm talking about forgotten religions—to say that they had the whole truth, they knew their mysteries. Now astronomy has defeated human ego—we no longer think we are very important in a hundred billion galaxies. I would like to see that happen in our knowledge of God. I don't think we know much more about God now than we knew about the hundred billion galaxies 2,000 years ago.

Sir John also commented along the same lines on his forty years as a trustee of Princeton Theological Seminary, and then described his experimental approach to a possible solution.

I've been a trustee of Princeton Seminary for forty years. They don't appropriate anything for research in the same sense that a hospital or a medical school would. The research in the Princeton budget is for archaeology and ancient scriptures, which is nice. But it doesn't really lead us to know a lot more about God in the end. Since I couldn't find any organization concentrating on progress in religion, I've undertaken that. I may not succeed. It may not be feasible for anybody, but that's what I'm focusing on. The first step, twenty-one years ago, was to offer prizes for progress in religion. The progress has come in different fields, and out of the twenty-three winners so far, five have been in *science* and religion.

I hope that we can do research on many subjects in science and religion. We can't hope to foresee where God will reveal himself. Bob Herrmann and I published a book called *The God Who Would Be Known*, with the idea that God is ready to reveal himself if we search with humility and in the right way. It never occurred to me to wonder *where* we should search—whether in astronomy or genetics or prayer or love. Almost no research has been done on love from a scientific standpoint, on its origin, nature, varieties, encouragement, or results. We are trying one thing after another to encourage people to do something that increases our knowledge of God, God's purposes, or God's love. Maybe 10 percent of the ideas we try will work. With that humble approach, it really never occurred to me to search, say, in astronomy and not in genetics.

Science Is Providing Empirical and Scholarly Approaches to New Ideas

John Templeton has become convinced that true progress in our seeking knowledge of God must take into account the incredible growth of our knowledge in the sciences. Science has revealed in the past few decades a universe of awesome size and complexity, and now it is some scientists who are speaking out about the theological implications of these revelations. Professor Paul Davies of the University of Adelaide, a winner of the Templeton Prize for Progress in Religion, is one of the first of many scientists impressed with the unmistakable appearance of meaning and purpose in this new picture of our universe. And coupling this new theological impulse with the power of the empirical approach so essential to science would seem to provide a new and fruitful avenue of discovery for the theological enterprise as well. What Sir John envisages is nothing less than a supplemental theology, born out of this progressive exploratory approach, a new experimental theology to add to the wonderful testimony of holy scriptures! And such a program would surely be worthy of support at something like the magnitude of our researches in the natural sciences. Again in *The Second Opinion* article he says:

> We are terribly ignorant. We should be anxious to learn, to experiment, to discover a little more about God. We should listen to anybody who thinks he knows something about God. More than a billion dollars a day are spent on scientific research. If one-tenth of that were spent on research in spiritual subjects, that would be a hundred million dollars a day. That would be visionary.

Prizes for Papers in Humility Theology

To promote this exciting vision, John Templeton began a program of prizes to encourage theologians and scientists to think and write and influence others in this new direction for progress in religion. An early step was to compile a directory of scholars writing and publishing in the interface between science and religion, and this compilation, carried out at the Center of Theological Inquiry in Princeton, revealed more than eight hundred scholars who were working in the general field. For the support of this endeavor, John Templeton went to his long-term friend and colleague Dr. James I. McCord, former president of Princeton Seminary and at that time chairman of the Center. He also recruited Professor Harold Nebelsick of Louisville Presbyterian Theological Seminary, a pioneer in the dialogue between theologians and scientists, to assist him in editing the volume. Sadly, Harold Nebelsick died suddenly on March 26, 1989 and the volume was eventually completed by John Webster, a Princeton Seminary student, and published in 1992. John Templeton provided $50,000 to support this work.

A second publication in support of this program has been the newsletter of the Humility Theology Information Center, *Progress in Theology,* of which I have been editorial co-ordinator. Our major involvement has been the publication of abstracts of winning papers, some two dozen in the course of the last three years. During this period we have received numerous letters and some manuscripts from our readers, many accompanied by pleas to help in the publication of new ideas in the area of theology and science. In reviewing the nature of these requests and the character of the manuscripts, we have come to realize that scholarship and the normal structure of publication, with its attendant research into the ideas of others and required peer review, is an essential ingredient of publication in humility theology. In the editorial for the March 1994 issue of *Progress in Theology* we said:

> One of the difficulties in any publishing endeavor is deciding which of many ideas should be presented in a specific forum. Ideas about progress in theology are no exception, and our editorial office has been favored with a rather bewildering array of papers presenting new concepts or old concepts in new

forms. Our difficulty is even more acute than usual because, on the one hand, we wish to encourage novelty and creativity, but on the other hand, we feel that such ideas should be somehow anchored to the world of scholarship.

The approach we have taken thus far in our program of publication is to invite material from recognized scholars, and particularly from those whose ideas and concepts have undergone editorial and peer scrutiny. Those of us who have a scientific background are very aware of the importance of interaction with colleagues and of a thorough literature search in the course of formulating new hypotheses. The subsequent submission of our best effort to a refereed journal is the most important step of all.

Some have argued that there are no avenues of publication for papers with progressive ideas about religion, but our experience suggests that that is rarely the case for well-thought-out and thoroughly documented papers. Publications that accept this type of material can be found by reviewing the journals listed in the publications of authors included in *Who's Who in Theology and Science,* published in 1992 by Winthrop Publishing Company (Framingham, Mass., ISBN: 1-879302-00-4). The importance of publication has also been emphasized in another program of the Center: The Call for Papers on Humility Theology. The Center's advisory board has strongly recommended that only papers published in scholarly, refereed science and religion journals be considered for awards in this program.

A second avenue that potential authors should consider is the critical interaction with a group of interested scholarly individuals. Membership in one of the science/religion organizations listed in Directory C of *Who's Who in Theology and Science* is an excellent way to develop a group for such interaction. For academicians, another approach is to interact with students by developing a rather open-ended course in science and religion. The Humility Theology Information Center is conducting a program for the development of academic courses in which science and religion are taught together. Here the emphasis is placed on a balanced treatment of the two disciplines, again with an effort to promote good scholarship.

The tension between the ideas of an individual and the collective views of a scholarly community will surely always be with us. Perhaps, as an example of humility theology, we need willingly to subject our most cherished ideas and convictions to the evidence of the past and the criticism of the current community of scholars. It is our hope that by this mechanism not all novel and original thinking will be suppressed, but rather that new ideas in theology will by their sheer power and grandeur find acceptance and become one means toward a new, spiritual Renaissance.

The Program of Prizes for Papers in Humility Theology was announced in 1991 with the following criteria.

1. Because of the importance of current science, the paper must either be documented to be in press or have been published in the past three years in a reputable scientific or theological journal.
2. The paper will be judged for an award on the basis of its contribution to our greater understanding and appreciation of the new climate of humility engendered by the sciences, and the theological openness which that awareness demands. The paper should of course be scholarly in its approach and coherent in its delivery. Papers should be between 2,000 and 10,000 words in length.

The announcement was mailed with a covering letter to the people in *Who's Who in Theology and Science,* and advertisements were placed in several science-theology journals, including *Zygon, Perspectives on Science and Christian Faith,* and *Science and Christian Belief.* Sixty-four authors submitted 130 papers in this first year of the program. Twelve papers were awarded prizes.

In the second year of the competition, we saw a definite improvement in the number and quality of submissions. More than 100 authors submitted 131 papers, 47 of which qualified for an award. In the third program, 65 papers were submitted and 35 prizes were awarded. The lower number involved in the third year is generally attributed to the fact that a new program inviting academics to submit courses in science and religion was running concurrently, and this new emphasis clearly diverted the attention of some potential "Call for Papers" participants.

Professor Howard Van Till of Calvin College, one of the judges of the first three programs, undertook direction of the fourth program. The emphasis broadened to include a second area of humility theology, the constructive interaction of religion and the health sciences. According to Professor Van Till, the criteria for this enlarged program will have the following domains of concern:

- Epistemological concerns—assessing the possibility, character, or extent of progress toward knowledge in theology, religion, science, and their mutual interactions;
- Empirical concerns—assessing the probative force of empirical investigation in the evaluation of theories regarding the mutual relevance of theology/religion and the sciences;
- Methodological concerns—assessing the methodologies appropriate to research on the relationships among theology, religion, and the sciences; and
- Constructive exploration—constructing, in a manner both creative and intellectually responsible, a novel perspective or way for growing in our understanding of God, ourselves, and the vast universe in which we live. This constructive exploration might well constitute one's response to the question, "Is it not possible that the unseen (the full array of spiritual realities that are not directly perceivable by our senses) is far more vast than the seen (the physical realities that can be sensibly perceived)?"

As we look at the results, it is instructive to realize that we have accessed a very large number of theological and scientific journals and involved a large number of scholars in this Papers in Humility Theology Program. In 1993 the winning papers were published in thirty-four different scholarly journals, and in 1994, twenty-six different journals were represented. Furthermore, the majority of papers came from theological faculty, indicating some attention by theology and religion departments to the possibilities of humility theology. Admittedly there is still much to be done, but it would seem that influencing theological scholarship may be part of the 10 percent of ideas that Sir John thinks may work.

CHAPTER 6

Discovering the "Laws of Life"

One of Sir John Templeton's major goals in his quest for progress in religion has been to deepen the spiritual training of high school and college students worldwide. His view of spirituality, however, goes well beyond Sunday school teaching or college classes in religion. Rather, he sees a need for a broad-based emphasis on "Laws of Life," spiritual laws that have served as guidelines for countless generations of people in all cultures and political settings. These laws, he says, have been deeply embedded in human history, with a similar kind of permanence and given-ness as the physical laws that appear to govern our universe. For example, he visualizes the Golden Rule, as taught by Jesus in the Sermon on the Mount—"do unto others as you would have others do unto you"—as a universally accepted law to live by. Agreed on in the three monotheistic religions, Judaism, Christianity and Islam, it is also proposed by all of the Eastern religions and philosophies. Many other spiritual laws have this same kind of acceptance, and they have been the mainstay of countless successful political, business, and professional leaders all over the world. The problem, as Sir John sees it, is that these spiritual laws have gradually lost prominence in our educational systems. As societies have become more secular and more professionally oriented, the deeper teachings, which build character and moral strength, have been seriously crowded out.

A High School Essay Program

One of John Templeton's approaches to a solution began with a teenage essay contest in Franklin County, Tennessee, which was developed with the help of his niece and nephew, Becky and Handly Templeton. At a 1986 meeting of the Humility Theology Information Center advisory board John talked about the background of this emphasis.

> We started the essay contest on the spiritual "Laws of Life" some years ago in the county in Tennessee where I grew up and it had an amazing effect on that county. Because America may be the only nation in the world that forbids teaching religion in the schools we did not work through the schools. We just made it publicly known that teenage boys and girls could win cash by writing essays on how they planned to lead their future lives—the spiritual principles they were going to use in their lives.
>
> Two things made it work: one was the prizes—not large, $2,000 for the first prize with nine prizes scaled down to $100. We offered these twice a year. Students of that age get terribly excited about winning $100 or $1,000. This idea just swept the county with three-quarters of the students of that age writing essays twice a year on the spiritual principles they expected to use in their lives. But, in addition, the other working principle is this: we don't tell them the spiritual principles. We ask them to tell us! Now there's magic in that, because people of that age love to tell you, but they sometimes resent *your* telling them. It also causes them to think. If they have to think it up for themselves, they understand it better than if they just read about it in a book. Also, they go to their parents and say "tell me what are the spiritual laws of life." Some of the parents have to think more than they would otherwise. It's the same with the teachers—they ask their teachers and the teachers have to think. Following the writing period the prize-winning essays are announced on the local radio and in the local newspapers. Then

we put on a banquet at the country club and give out honors and plaques to the prize winners.

This program is having just a transforming effect on this county. It's been so remarkable that we've prepared a handbook about how to organize an essay program. A similar program was started in Bradley County, Tennessee, and this has also been very successful. It was also started in Jackson, Mississippi, and in 1997 over four dozen other localities are imitating this program.

Dr. Jack Templeton, Sir John's son, added his own enthusiasm:

Students who were in many cases not doing well in their classes found for the first time that the assignment was not directed at them but that the idea was to come out of them. One set of parents said, "Our daughter hasn't talked to us in two years and now she's interested in things that are important to our family." So families are really growing in the experience. Some students not particularly distinguished in their academics and some who were even disruptive in their classes became focused on the idea that someone cared about what they had to say. These students were often not those who were the most polished writers. Their grammar and punctuation may not have been perfect, but sometimes the content was so deep that often someone who was at best a C student could be a prize winner. This did a tremendous amount for their self-esteem, and with the public recognition both at the dinners and in being identified in the school newspapers, the students' own academic achievement began to go up because they found a measure of appreciation for their own productivity. . . .

. . . Our real hope is that this will be like dropping pebbles in a pond; that there will be a big ripple effect so that with the help of a new managing director of the program we can take this idea to centers around the country. We will talk to individuals and organizations like Rotary Club to undertake this with their county or their school district. Part of what has worked well in Franklin County is that it has brought together public schools and private schools to interrelate in this project. There's a lot to be gained in the local areas when people realize that there's more hope and concern in the younger generation.

As for John's own part, being brought up in the hill country of Tennessee was probably not a bad way to gain strength and direction for life. For example, in the farming community where John Templeton grew up, truthfulness was a law of life. Your word was your bond. People of character would never promise something and then go back on their word. A contract between two parties did not have to be put in writing. There was no need for a court or a judge to enforce it. Civilization, as it was then perceived by many, was a place where the handshake was sacred. Sir John says that doors and windows in his home town of Winchester were never locked. For that matter, any hardware store would sell skeleton keys that worked in 90 percent of the door locks. Every home had a Bible—sometimes as the only book. Motion picture theaters showed only films that taught ethics—the hero always won and in the end the villain always lost. Prohibition precluded any home having alcoholic drinks under penalty of jail. And in his seventeen years growing up in Winchester, he remembers only one person who was a drug addict. The saying of that time was probably true as well that "nine out of ten Franklin County ladies are intimate with only one man in a lifetime."

But John Templeton had much more of a positive influence toward character building than any of his Winchester friends. His father was a paragon of thrift, yet was ever willing to sponsor the worthwhile projects John had thought up. And his mother was quite unique, being very well educated for the time and for rural Tennessee. After seven years of study at Winchester Normal College, she then tutored for two years for a wealthy Texas family before returning to Winchester to eventually marry Harvey Templeton. Recall that it was Vella who became interested in the Unity Movement, with its emphasis on the positive, on possibilities, and on the virtues of material prosperity. It was Unity that emphasized "thought control," the ability to discipline yourself, to focus your mind on those things that were positive and most productive. Physical healing, wealth, inner peace—almost anything was possible if your mental processes were in tune with the great divine principles of the universe. The capacity for greatness was within, where God was ever present.

Acting on these principles, Harvey and Vella Templeton gave young John almost total freedom to do what he thought best. He was never given advice about ethics, religion, or conduct though he was active in the Cumberland Presbyterian Church and had ready access to the literature of the Unity Movement and to a set of the *Book of Knowledge Encyclopedia.*

Only once in John Templeton's school career was he asked if he'd done his homework assignment. Because young Templeton found Latin a difficult subject, his mother, who had studied Latin for seven years, would sometimes help him. She once asked him if he'd finished his work. He hesitated but finally told her, "Mother, all my life I've gotten nothing but As. Even in Latin. Not a single grade lower than an A. So please leave it up to me. I love you for your solicitude, but you needn't worry." She never asked him again.

John Templeton understood the virtues of promptness and perseverance at a tender age. When he was in the first grade, he took his report card home and showed his father, with understandable pride, that all of the subjects were marked A. His father was very pleased and said that he would like to set up a contest. On each of John's half-year reports that showed nothing lower than A, he would give his son a bale of cotton. Each time there was a grade lower than an A, however, John would have to give his father a bale of cotton.

The theory was that the son would wind up owing his father many, many bales of cotton, which would be a lesson to John. But the older Templeton did not reckon with his son's will power, desire to succeed, and his early ability to get the most out of the minutes in an hour. He worked hard at his lessons, he was always prompt with them, and he went through grammar school and high school without a single grade below an A. Thus, eleven years later, his father owed him twenty-two bales of cotton. But then in the Great Depression, when John's father could give no more tuition money beyond supporting his first year at Yale, John refused to accept those twenty-two bales.

John's mother was in many ways a superb teacher of self-reliance. One summer, for example, when John was twelve, his mother loaded him, his fifteen-year-old brother, and a couple of cousins in the car and took them on an extensive two-month trip throughout the northeast. They traveled about one hundred miles a day, camped out, and did their own cooking. But this was not a parent-controlled vacation. The kids were in charge just as much as Vella Templeton, with each person participating in selecting the routes and activities and setting up the day's campsite.

Even though they had a lot of fun, the trip was by no means merely a relaxed, carefree sort of affair. Every moment was scheduled, and myriads of stimulating sights and experiences were packed into each day. For example, every time they arrived in a big metropolitan area like Washington, New York, or Philadelphia, they would hit all the museums—and that meant every room on every floor of every major museum.

It was a hectic two months, but such high-powered activity, combined with intensive learning experiences, was what young John learned to expect and love as a boy. And that trip served to set the stage for still another summer adventure a few years later.

When John was sixteen, his mother loaded up the car again—this time with John, Harvey, Jr., and one classmate—and they headed west. Their goal: to see *everything* west of the Mississippi—all the historic sites, national parks, national monuments, and the Pacific Ocean. Again, they were gone about two months, and they camped out every night.

This kind of intensive study of one part of the country or one area of knowledge was part of a regular pattern in John's childhood. It not only instilled in him self-confidence, but also a love for travel and an outward look, which in later years gave him the advantage in international investing.

John's youth was a time of great activity—crammed with projects and experiments and meaningful learning experiences. It is not surprising that he covets this self-discovery for the young people of today! Noteworthy too is his avoidance of entertainment through television or radio; he estimates that in eighty-four years he has watched less than eighty-four hours of television, except for spiritual programs.

The Honor Roll for Character-Building Colleges

In 1989 Sir John Templeton initiated a second program for character building and moral development—this time in the nation's colleges and universities. His idea was to select approximately one hundred schools whose educational programs and campus activities showed the greatest commitment to the personal growth and moral development of their students. Several approaches were considered.

1. Selection could be made by a survey of opinion leaders like college presidents, each voting for a small number of institutions that they believed to stand out among the hundreds of applicant institutions.
2. Review of a set of institutional criteria obtained by way of a questionnaire submitted by each applicant institution.
3. Review of data submitted by each institution about the beliefs and behavior of its students.

It was decided that the first option should be tried first, given the proven success of this approach in other national educational surveys. For example the *U.S. News and World Report* national survey, which periodically rates America's best colleges, uses the opinion leader approach, and its results are widely accepted in the academic community. Regardless of the approach taken, one of the clear benefits of the review process is that each institution learns a great deal about what others are doing in terms of character building and personal moral development. Specific courses dedicated to personal ethics, applied ethics, the psychology of human development, moral reasoning, or human values are often listed. Programs are often outlined for community involvement, overseas missions, and campus ministries for the handicapped and those with pressing personal problems.

In 1995 the applicant institutions were asked to respond to the following five criteria:

- Encourages students to explore an individual moral reasoning process;
- Fosters positive attitudes and overall well-being;
- Encourages spiritual growth and moral values;
- Promotes community-building values; and
- Advocates drug-free lifestyle.

The Foundation received applications from 325 institutions. About half listed specific courses in character building and personal ethics. Most institutions were religiously-affiliated; only about 20 percent of the 325 were state-supported or private secular institutions. However, these nonreligious schools had a higher proportion of courses or programs in personal and applied ethics. In 1995 there were 124 schools on the Honor Roll.

Future Plans for Academic Courses Emphasizing Spiritual "Laws of Life"

John Templeton plans to develop a full-scale program to encourage courses in character building and spiritual development in the nation's colleges and universities. A survey is under way to assess the number of courses of this kind currently being taught. Academic catalogs are being examined for courses offered in the departments of psychology, philosophy, religious studies, and sociology, which have titles like the following:

- Personal Ethics;
- Applied Ethics;
- Ethics in Health Sciences;
- Personal Development;
- Human Values;
- Ethics and Philosophy;
- Psychology of Human Development; and
- Moral Reasoning.

Course listings are also being sought under special programs with the following types of names: "Honors Program," "General Education," "Freshman Seminar," "Capstone Courses," and "Enrichment Program."

The approach is similar to the Foundation's program for the development of courses on science and religion. Institutions listing courses in spiritual development are invited to submit their courses to a competition with prizes for perhaps the ten best courses meeting criteria of character building and personal moral and spiritual development. The ten winning courses are used as models in a larger prize program to encourage the development of academic courses worldwide.

One of the major values of a collegiate program in spiritual development is that it meets a need for recognition of teachers in the human sciences and the humanities who generally receive little recognition for their interest in spiritual development. The guidelines of the Foundation program encouraging courses in science and religion has as its focus the relationship between the physical sciences and religion. Courses concentrating on the human sciences—sociology or psychology—and on ethics are appropriately not favored. However, a program of support for courses in spiritual development easily embraces courses of this type if they are modified to emphasize spiritual "Laws of Life." In this way the two programs can be complementary and mutually supportive.

It is to be hoped that in the future other foundations that are interested in education will follow the lead of the Templeton Foundation in emphasizing spiritual values on the campus.

Discovering the "Laws of Life"

In another chapter of this book we talked about some of the "Laws of Life," which John Templeton first described in *The Humble Approach*. We also mentioned the compilation of two hundred spiritual laws in his book, *Discovering the Laws of Life*. Sir John is quick to point out that this is a tentative list. Some of these laws doubtless will not prove to be generally valid, and they will be set aside. But research may show that a significant number of the laws have scientific validity and these will become part of a more widely accepted book called *Worldwide Laws of Life*. Some of the research data supporting the laws' validity are included in this new edition, for specific use in academic courses. As a proven textbook, it is hoped that *Worldwide Laws of Life* can find its way into accredited courses in some colleges and universities worldwide. Sir John even envisions the development of a "World Council on the Laws of Life" leading to a world view with educators and all the world's religions in agreement.

A Russian-language version of *Discovering the Laws of Life* for schools has been produced already. The two hundred "Laws of Life" in this version are coupled with quotations from the writings of famed Russian author Leo Tolstoy. There is also a British schools edition adapted for classroom use under the direction of Templeton Foundation trustee Dr. Russell Stannard of the Open University and Reverend Stephen Orchard of the Christian Education Movement in the United Kingdom. This book, called *Looking Inwards/Looking Outwards*, is produced for students of religious education (aged thirteen and up) in the British secondary schools to help them meet their legal requirement of 5 percent of religious education instruction in their daily course work through the twelfth school year. This includes an appendix with information for teachers and a series of work assignments for students.

Scientific verification of the "Laws of Life" has begun, with social psychologist Dr. David Myers of Hope College collaborating with Dr. Kevin Sharpe. Their goal is to identify twenty-five or more spiritual laws that can be stated in a form suitable for testing by scientific methodologies. It is hoped that many other scientists will be attracted to this cause in the future.

CHAPTER 7

Bringing Science and Religion Together on Campus

The Gap between Science and Religion

 John Templeton's enthusiasm for progress in spiritual information and research finds a challenging arena in the world's institutions of higher learning. Over the past century most of our universities and colleges have gradually shifted their allegiance from a religious world view to a scientific one. The scientific view most generally presented the world as a clock-like structure ruled by natural laws. Everything that happened seemed resolvable into cause and effect. There seemed no need for God. Objective science became the supreme arbiter of truth, the source of progress, the frontier subject. Religion came to be viewed as backward-looking, almost irrelevant to the modern age.

To Sir John, this was a sad and largely unrealistic state of affairs. The nine judges for the Templeton Prize for Progress in Religion awarded that prize on several occasions to university theology professors. This highlights the fact that there still were forward-looking pioneers in academic religion departments. Among them were Sir Sarvepalli Radhakrishnan, Oxford professor of eastern religion and ethics, who received the prize in 1975; Thomas Torrance, professor of Christian dogmatics at the University of Edinburgh, who received the prize in 1978; and Ralph Wendell Burhoe, professor of theology at the Meadville/Lombard Theological School's Center for Advanced Study in Chicago, who was awarded the prize in 1980. But these three prizes represented for John Templeton only a small token of his enthusiasm for progress in spiritual information and research.

In his 1981 book, *The Humble Approach,* Sir John talked about the enormous creative opportunities that lie before us and placed the blame for the present narrow outlook of most religious people squarely on human egotism. By contrast, he said, many or most natural scientists have displayed an open-minded, exploratory, tolerant, and searching attitude, and he strongly recommended that theologians could benefit from their example. In the introduction he writes:

> We are perched on the frontier of future knowledge. Even though we stand upon the enormous mountain of information collected over the last five centuries of scientific progress, we have only fleeting glimpses of the future. To a large extent, the future lies before us like a vast wilderness of unexplored reality. The God who created and sustained His evolving universe through eons of progress and development has not placed our generation at the tag end of the creative process. He has placed us at a new beginning. We are here for the future.
>
> Our role is crucial. As human beings we are endowed with mind and spirit. We can think, imagine, and dream. We can search for future trends through the rich diversity of human thought. God permits us in some ways to be co-creators with Him in His continuing act of creation.
>
> There is, however, a stumbling block: egotism. The closed-minded attitude of those who think they know it all inhibits future progress. Natural scientists, by and large, have overcome this hurdle. They are more open-minded. They research the natural wonders of the universe, devising new hypotheses, testing them, challenging old assumptions, competing with each other in professional rivalry. The physical future of human civilization is in their professional hands, guided by relatively tolerant and open minds.
>
> This is not equally true concerning our spiritual future. Some theologians, religious leaders, and lay people are

frequently blind to the obstacles they themselves erect. Many are not even aware that the spiritual future could, or should, be different from anything that has ever been before. Many do not realize that spiritual reality can be researched in ways similar to those used by natural scientists. Some do not want even to consider the possibilities of a future of progressively unfolding spiritual discoveries.

Why not? Many devoutly religious people are not devoutly humble. They do not admit their world view is limited. They are not open to suggestions that their personal theology might be incomplete. They do not entertain the notion that other religions have valuable insights to contribute to an understanding of God and His creation. When people take a more humble attitude, they welcome new ideas about the spirit just as they welcome new scientific ideas about how to cure headaches, how to heat and cool their homes, or how to develop natural resources.[1]

Sir John feels that the future of our spiritual understanding is far too important to be left in the hands of people of restricted vision or people who are preoccupied with protecting their turf. This period in our history is the blossoming time, when the human enterprise is bursting into flower and the growth of human knowledge is accelerating at an incredible pace. In *The Humble Approach* he writes:

> More than half of the scientists who ever lived are alive today. More than half of the discoveries in the natural sciences have been made in this century. More than half of the goods produced since the earth was born have been produced in the twentieth century. Over half the books ever written were written in the last half-century.[2]

Yet this explosion in our scientific knowledge has not brought about a conviction among most scientists that we have learned all there is to learn. There may be a few zealots like Stephen Hawking who suggest that we are approaching a theory of everything, which will bring the "end of physics" and "then we shall know the mind of God." But the vast majority of working scientists realize that we are only beginning to be aware of the extent of our ignorance. The past few decades have brought most scientists to a sense of awe and to a new humility. And some are once again looking at their science for philosophical and theological meaning, almost in the way many of the early scientists spoke of their scientific endeavors as opening the book of God's works.

Given this remarkable recent change in attitude among many scientists, John Templeton sees the stage set for a new dialogue between scientists, philosophers, and theologians, especially on university and college campuses. More than this, he sees the opportunity for the revitalization of religion, theology, and science departments. Given the new world that science has brought to us they should, he says, be the most exciting focus for new ideas and concepts in the university. All of this would be possible if we adopted a new spirit of humility, open to the God of a universe infinitely greater and more complex than we could ever have dreamed. Sir John gives us another side of this new challenge to theology in another chapter of *The Humble Approach*, titled "The New World of Time." In it he mentions Teilhard de Chardin's view of God's activity as a progression from the geosphere to the biosphere to the noosphere—the sphere of the mind—and then to a consummation in Omega Point. But, Sir John asks, what if there is no Omega Point, but rather yet other spheres and other worlds.

> The twentieth century after Christ may very well represent a new renaissance in human culture, a new embarcation into future cultures. Persons born in this century can hardly imagine the small amount of knowledge and the limited concept of the cosmos man had when the scriptures of all the five major religions were written. Do old scriptures need reinterpreting to accommodate an expanded notion of the universe?
>
> More important for theology is the expanded concept of history. When all the scriptures of all major religions were written, the history of the universe was conceived as only a few thousand years. Now geologists and paleontologists who

think in hundreds of millions of years read history in visible form sometimes more reliable than history books or scriptures. And cosmologists think in billions of years. Because light travels a hundred and eighty-six thousand miles a second, we can see the sun not as it is now, but as it was some eight minutes ago. We see some stars as they were when Christ was born. We see some galaxies as they were six million years ago. Such a revolution in our conceptions of time and history is beginning to shape our theology.

What existed before this universe began? What will exist after the sun has grown cold? After minerals there emerged plants, and after plants animals, and after animals there emerged minds; and minds began to participate in the creative process. What comes next? Is there evidence that minds are developing into even more miraculous spirits and souls? These are not only questions of science but also of theology—a new type of theology not yet taught in the seminaries.

Consider the cold, inert world of minerals, the throbbing world of life, the curious, searching realm of the intellect. What next? This may be the most important question facing us at the end of the twentieth century. To answer it, scientists are daily engaged in new scientific experiments that will help us know more about the vast unseen. Theologians, too, answering Chardin's call for a new religion, must begin to explore the vast unseen dimensions of our evolving universe; they must plumb the very "depths of God's own nature."[3]

In some ways, the university may be ready for a new dialogue between the sciences and the humanities—with special reference to religion. Robert Sollod, at Cleveland State University, has published an article in *The Chronicle of Higher Education* calling for a reconsideration of religion and spirituality as integral parts of college curricula in this era of curriculum reform.[4] Additionally, Stephen Cain, staff reporter for the *Ann Arbor News,* has reported on a conference at the University of Michigan that called for the reincorporation of values, ethics, morality, and organized religion into the life of the university. University regent Laurence Deitch said at that conference,

"There has been a breakdown of values in our society with little counter force from any point of view other than the religious right. Values can and should be taught at the university."[5]

John Templeton has proposed that we get more religion departments to take a scientific view of their subject, opening their minds to the new scientific discoveries with their challenging voices for theology. He has proposed a number of ways that this might be encouraged by the Templeton Foundation. One of the most promising so far is a program to encourage the development of new and improved courses joining science and religion.

The Science & Religion Course Program

Begun in 1994, the first phase of the program involved the identification of academic courses in science and religion that could serve as models or guides for faculty interested in the development of new and improved courses in institutions worldwide. Sir John chose the approach of a broad sweep, surveying all catalog offerings in colleges, universities, and seminaries in the United States and Canada. The search team found 943 science and religion courses. Questionnaires were sent to the course managers, department heads, or deans, requesting syllabi and additional information about the courses. Prizes of $5,000 each were offered for the best five courses identified. The response was surprisingly meager, with only some fifty questionnaires returned, but among the courses identified were a number of excellent quality, based upon the following criteria:

1. Solid scholarship
   a. Good syllabus, bibliography, reading list, library resources
   b. Inclusion of philosophical and historical aspects

Sir John Templeton reading the *Wall Street Journal* at the exact North Pole, July 27, 1996. Russian icebreaker *Yamal* is in background.

Relatives attending Sir John's eightieth birthday celebration, 1992. *Front row (l to r)*: Hillary Brooks, Admiral Winston Folk, USN Ret., Sir John Templeton, Irene Templeton, Gregory Carrol, Jewel Templeton, Cameron Brooks. *From second to back (l to r)*: Colin Brooks, Sander Brooks, Irene Reynolds Butler, Anne Dudley Zimmerman, Wendy Brooks, Virginia Templeton, Amy Butler, Heather Templeton, Christopher Templeton, Mrs. Gäbriel Flynn, Gäbriel Flynn, Josephine Templeton, Jennifer Templeton, Ann Cameron, Jennifer Cameron, Gail Zimmerman, Renee Zimmerman, Richard Sidman, Jill Sidman, Lauren Templeton, Rhonda Zimmerman, Eva Zimmerman, Harvey Templeton III, Becky Templeton, Jason Flynn, Derek Dietz. *Top row (l to r)*: Michael Zimmerman, Malcolm Butler, John M. Templeton Jr., Handly Templeton

Managers of Templeton Foundation, Bahamas, 1997: Mrs. Mena Griffiths, Sir John Templeton, and Mrs. Mary Walker

Templeton Foundations staff, Radnor, Pennsylvania 1997 (*l to r*): Anne Heilman, Karyl Wittlinger, Bryant Kirkland, Aideen Quigley, Judith Marchand, Fran Schapperle, Charles Harper, Joanna Hill, John Templeton, Jr., Arthur Schwartz, Laura Molina, Linda Kelly, Andrea Beckerman, Joann DiIullo, Pat Laird. Not pictured: Pam Lairdieson and Patricia Hotz.

Harvey Maxwell Templeton, 1930

Vella Handly Templeton, 1908

Harvey Templeton, Jr. *(left)* and
John Marks Templeton, 1914.

John Marks Templeton ca. 1916

John Marks Templeton,
1930

Judith Dudley Folk Templeton
wedding, Nashville, Tennessee
1937

Portrait of John
Marks Templeton,
1950

For my dear friend
John Templeton —
ever as kind as
he is wise —
which is saying
a lot, indeed!
All the best,
always,

John Templeton and Louis Rukeyser, 1992

Board of Directors of Templeton Investment Funds. *Front row (l to r)*: Baron von Diergardt, Harold Siebens, John Galbraith, Sir John Templeton, William James, Lloyd Blachford, John Goldstone. *Back row (l to r)*: Bruce Clark, Bruce McGowan, Mark Holowesko, Jay Bradshaw, Harry Kuch, Gary Motyl, Leroy Paslay, Tom Hansberger, Dr. John M. Templeton, Jr., Richard Tottenham.

The growth of the Templeton Growth Fund, Ltd., as compared to the Cost of Living Index.

Portrait of John Marks Templeton
at home, 1980

Portrait of Irene Reynolds Butler
Templeton, 1961

One branch of the
Templeton family.
Seated (l to r): Pina,
Heather, and Irene.
Standing (l to r): John
M. Templeton, Jr. and
John Marks Temple-
ton, 1978

    c. Emphasis on current scientific developments, primarily in the natural sciences; special emphasis on physics, cosmology, genetics, neural sciences, and environmental science

2. A balanced treatment of the science/religion dialogue
   a. Both scientific and religious perspectives represented
   b. Emphasis on historical perspective
3. An attitude of intellectual humility
   a. Presentations exploratory rather than dogmatic and critical
   b. Evidence that students are encouraged to ask questions and that adequate discussion time is provided
4. Adequate evaluation of course
   a. Acceptance by the institution
   b. Evidence of significant course enrollment
   c. Indication of history of the course
      1. Number of years taught
      2. Course enrollment over the years
      3. Type of student—undergraduates, graduate students, major fields

The five course managers were awarded $5,000 prizes and asked to prepare six-page summaries of their winning courses. A sixth course, offered by Robert Russell, one of the judges of the program, was also included. These six course summaries became the foundation for the larger program to follow.

A description of the model course winners and their courses was published in the science-religion journal *Zygon*. It was written by freelance science writer Margaret Wertheim and appeared in the September 1995 issue (vol.30, no. 3., 491–500).

The second phase of the program was announced in June of 1994 in the various science and religion journals and newsletters: *Zygon, Perspectives on Science and Christian Faith, Science and Christian Belief, the Journal for the Scientific Study of Religion, Science and Religion News,* and *Progress in Theology.* In addition, personal letters were sent to some five hundred faculty listed in *Who's Who in Theology and Science.*

Sir John was eager to get participation by a broad segment of the academic science and religion communities, so he made the generous offer of up to one hundred prizes of $10,000 each—$5,000 for the course manager and $5,000 for the institution—for new or improved courses that followed the criteria that had been set for the model courses. Winners were required to attend an all-expenses-paid workshop on course design the following summer, with the intent that a network of faculty in the field could be established and liaison with the Foundation maintained.

Then in September, Sir John decided that we should add an additional workshop, this time for applicants who might be new to this interdisciplinary area but interested enough to travel at their own expense. I recall questioning if people would come to Tallahassee, Florida, to Florida State University, at their own expense. Sir John was quite sure they would, given the incentive of the $10,000 prize, half of which was designated for the institution. Surely institutions would support the travel expense, if it represented an investment toward the award. And of course he was right! Despite the lateness of the announcement and the cost of travel, more than 150 faculty inquired and nearly 80 faculty attended the workshop.

By every criterion, the workshop was a success. There was excellent leadership by Robert Russell and John Albright, an adequate staff, superb facilities, an enthusiastic welcome by the president of the university and the dean, and an atmosphere of excitement as like-minded faculty (who thought they were alone in their interest in religion and science) found each other. The attendees' evaluations were very positive. Furthermore, they gave every indication of being teachable—even the few who had been involved with a science-religion course for many years. They certainly were very appreciative of the Templeton Foundation's vision! And perhaps of most importance, more than half of the attendees were from secular schools, and more than half had never taught a formal science-religion course.

The response to the second phase of the award program was equally enthusiastic. A total of 184 applications were received and 173 were reviewed for an award. An analysis of the applicants is presented in Table 1.

The largest number of courses, seventy-two, came from faculty in religion and theology departments, amounting to 42 percent of the total. Science departments accounted for 18 percent and philosophy departments 16 percent of the total. Of the remainder, the largest percentage originated in various interdisciplinary programs. More revealing perhaps, the percentage of applications from secular institutions was greatest for interdisciplinary programs, suggesting that faculty in secular institutions intending to initiate courses in science and religion may find good possibilities in the great variety of interdisciplinary programs that are developing at secular institutions. Overall, 43 percent of the applications came from secular institutions.

The table also presents the ratio of new to improved courses submitted for awards. Applicants for new courses

TABLE 1

Phase II Applications

	Total Appns.	% of Total	Number from Secular Instns.	% from Secular Instns.	Ratio of New/ Improv
Science Depts.	32	18	13	41	19/13
Philosophy Depts.	27	16	13	48	20/7
Religion & Theology Depts.	72	42	21	29	40/32
History Depts.	13	7	8	62	4/9
Interdisciplinary Programs	29	17	20	70	22/7
Total	173	100	75	43	105/68

predominated, with philosophy departments and interdisciplinary programs applying primarily with new courses while science, religion, and history departments brought almost equal numbers of new and improved courses to the competition.

The number of courses from foreign institutions, presented in Table 2, is also significant. Overall, thirty-seven of the applicants were from outside the United States.

Finally, among the applicants to the award program were a number of prestige institutions in the United States and overseas. We have received applications from such noted American institutions as Carnegie-Mellon, Dartmouth, Duke, Emory, Florida State, Indiana, Miami, Pennsylvania, Wisconsin, and Princeton Seminary. Foreign representatives include Bonn, Cambridge, Heidelberg, London, Oxford, the Russian Academy of Science, and Sydney.

Ninety-seven courses were chosen for an award. Course winners were required to attend one of three summer workshops: in Berkeley at the Center for Theology and the Natural Sciences; in Chicago at the Chicago Center for Religion and Science at the Lutheran School of Theology; and in the Boston area at Gordon College and Harvard University. All three workshops held highly successful sessions where awardees presented their courses in the form of a poster attached to a bulletin board and answered questions during a one hour

TABLE 2

Phase II Applications from Foreign Institutions

Australia 1	New Zealand 1
Brazil 1	Poland 1
Canada 8	Russia 1
Finland 1	Spain 1
Germany 4	South Africa 1
Iran 1	Taiwan 1
Ireland 1	United Kingdom 12
Netherlands 2	
	Total 37

period. In addition, visits and lectures were arranged for appropriate museums and libraries in each of the workshop areas to provide enrichment experiences and to illustrate the breadth of the science-religion relationship. For example, at the Boston area workshop, Harvard professor Owen Gingerich arranged a special lecture-demonstration at the Harvard Science Center's Museum of Historical Scientific Instruments and a special lecture and dinner at the Boston Museum of Science with museum president David Ellis.

On the strength of this favorable experience with the Phase II program, Sir John approved a second year of the award program at the same level—one hundred prizes of $10,000 each, again divided equally between the course manager and the institution. I also proposed to him that we set up six regional centers to hold workshops and network the participants in the program. Four of the centers would be responsible for the workshops in Berkeley, Chicago, Boston, and Tallahassee as before. However, two new centers would be added—one in Oxford, England to handle British, European, and South African participants, and one in Toronto to focus on Canadian participants. There would be winter workshops in Berkeley, Tallahassee, and Oxford and summer workshops in Berkeley and Oxford but also in Chicago, Boston, and Toronto. The budget for this expanded workshop program reached almost a million dollars, making the total cost of the entire Phase III program almost two million dollars. Nevertheless, Sir John approved the proposal, and the award program gave out one hundred more prizes in 1996, and another ninety-seven awards in 1997. An advertiement for the entire program is included in Appendix F at the back of this book.

Part II

The Making of a
World-Class Investor

CHAPTER 8

The Winchester Years

Sir John Templeton drove a small red rental car out of the long sweeping drive of the big brick house at 600 South High Street in Winchester, Tennessee, and proceeded south down High Street. It was the beginning of two days of travel down memory lane—to recount for me some of his experiences growing up in a small town in middle Tennessee. The big brick house had been built by John's father for his parents, Dr. John Wiley Templeton of Beech Grove, Tennessee and Susan Jones Templeton, formerly of Canton, Mississippi. Dr. Templeton had received his one year of medical training in Nashville, and had been a regimental surgeon in the Confederate Army during the Civil War. After the war he practiced general medicine for some forty years in Wartrace, Tennessee and then retired to live in Winchester.

The first stop in our trip was almost immediate; the house next door, where John grew up. It was a large stone house built by John's father for Vella Handly two years after they were married. Harvey Templeton and Vella Handly had begun their married life living with the older Templetons, and when she moved to the new house, she made the most of it. The house was set closer to the road, and had a long low double limestone wall designed as a planter with an earth-filled center. Vella's love of flowers took the form of a cascade of hanging petunias, which draped the full length of the wall.

There were six acres of land in all, including an entire acre of flowers, as well as pecan trees and plantings of a variety of vegetables and fruit. Just beyond the Templeton property in the old days was a field of sedge and wild flowers, which attracted many butterflies, the collection of which became one of John's many hobbies and continues to this day. Turning right at the end of the block, we soon encountered a series of small houses built by John's father; John (age eleven) and his brother Harvey (age fourteen) had wired the houses as part of the construction work. Both boys were remarkably knowledgeable about electricity, which along with such things as auto repair, gardening, astronomy, butterfly collecting, hunting, fishing, and travel made the Templetons a very interesting family.

At the next corner we turned right again and soon reached the town cemetery. At a site near the road was a well-kept plot with the graves of John's father, mother, and maternal grandfather. The plot was originally purchased by Vella's family. Her father, Robert Clinton Handly, had been a businessman in Winchester, with a busy grain mill on Boiling Fork Creek. The Handlys were also prominent politically. John's maternal grandmother, Elizabeth Marks, was the sister of Colonel Albert Marks, governor of Tennessee. John can even boast of a Revolutionary War hero, Virginia-born Samuel Handly, whose parents emigrated from northern Ireland in 1740. Samuel fought the Cherokee Indians, who were believed to have been incited by the British at the beginning of the Revolution, and later he was involved in a decisive victory over British forces at King's Mountain, North Carolina. He is buried in Belvedere, Tennessee, and his tombstone records that he was also "a member of the first convention that formed the Constitution of the State of Tennessee."

Just after we passed the cemetery, Sir John pointed out a row of low-income houses on the other side of the street. Several of these were built by his father with lumber he purchased when the old courthouse was torn down. According to John, this was a bit of fulfilled prophecy. Like John's father, John's Uncle Jess was also a lawyer in Winchester, with offices in the Farmer's National Bank building where John's father had his offices. "Uncle Jess was several times judge of the county court. I helped in the hard-fought political campaigns when he was elected judge and was always surprised that the judge's salary was only $900 a year. One of his opponents, Judge Frank Lynch, (the father of John's main high school sweetheart, Katrine Lynch) told people 'Do not elect Jess because if you do, his brother Harvey will wind up owning the courthouse.' Sure enough, a few years later during the Great Depression the federal government made a grant to Franklin County for the purpose of building a new courthouse. Accordingly, the old courthouse was put up for demolition and auction and was bought by my father, who used the materials to build rental houses on the edge of Winchester."

A little farther along, the road dips down and to the left, to the old railroad station and a junk yard, which was the site of another of John's father's enterprises, a cotton gin. The location was referred to locally as Gin Bottom, and it was here that some one hundred local farmers brought their cotton to be ginned for two dollars per bale. As many as two thousand bales were ginned there in a single season in the 1920s. Mr. Harvey, as John's father was often called, also stored cotton for the government and over the years bought a number of farms at auction. These enterprises, along with his practice as a self-educated lawyer, allowed Harvey Templeton to provide a quite adequate standard of living for his family. Although not rich, his was certainly one of the more prosperous families in Franklin County in John's childhood years. When Buicks were first sold in Franklin County in 1916, his uncle bought the first one and his father the second.

Continuing our journey, we turned right and climbed the hill from Gin Bottom into the center of Winchester. The typical square, with courthouse in the center, seemed like many others I've seen in recent years. There was still the old theater on one corner and a few restaurants, jewelers, and banks interspersed with a number of vacant storefronts. Back in John's childhood days, this was the center of activities. Vella Templeton's brother owned a dry goods store here and Vella worked in the store as the maker of ladies hats.

Just a block from the center of town we passed the Knies hardware store. It was across the street from an abandoned building which had been, during John's childhood, the Knies blacksmith shop, complete with forge, where John watched horseshoes being "hammered out in the old-fashioned way." Once more around the square, we turned onto Dinah Shore Boulevard, named after the singer-actress, the other famous person of that generation, who hails from Winchester, Tennessee. Dinah's family ran the only clothing store in Winchester when John was growing up. John tells the story of meeting Dinah many years later, in 1988, at a special county homecoming celebration. Sitting together at the head table at dinner, Dinah remarked about John's fame as a world-class investor, perhaps implying, as so often happens, that he might give her a hot tip about the stock market. He responded, "If you promise not to ask me about investments, I'll promise not to sing!"

It was on that same occasion that John announced the idea of a "Laws of Life" essay contest for Franklin County.

Just after turning onto the boulevard, John pointed out the old jail house, now a museum, and just below it the pond that was part of Boiling Fork Creek. Here he went frog hunting as a kid. A mile upstream on that creek Vella Templeton's father had his corn grinding mill. All of that is changed, John said, because of the damming of the Elk River and its tributaries as part of the huge Tennessee Valley Authority project.

After some brief shopping on the boulevard we returned to the big brick house on South High Street, now the home of

John's brother, Harvey Templeton, Jr., to spend the afternoon and dinner with the family.

Reminiscing at the Old Homestead with Harvey and Jewel Templeton

Harvey Templeton is John's older brother, a former nursery-man turned racing car driver and now retired. Almost his first words to me were "sit down and reveal the meaning of life." It was clear from the conversation that followed that he is not the man of faith that John is. He sees religion as many do, as judgmental and austere, and sees himself as something of a free spirit. One would certainly have to credit him for showing a lot of courage and daring, leaving a prosperous nursery business in his late fifties to begin a career as a racing car builder and racer. Nor was his wife Jewel at all a hindrance in this new career, she being a climber and skier and something of a daredevil behind the wheel. They later took me out to the "smokehouse," which has long since exchanged its role of curing ham and bacon for that of a machine shop and garage for Harvey's last Ford Formula 4 racing car and for Jewel's Lotus sports car. Back in the house are racing pictures—in one Harvey is arm in arm with Paul Newman with their racers behind them—and quite a few cups commemorating successful races at Daytona Beach and elsewhere. It is easy to see that Harvey and John both inherited some rather creative genes, though John's early love for engineering in the form of refurbishing old cars, wiring houses, and putting on "electric shows" was gradually shifted in the direction of entrepreneurship—raising cash crops, selling fireworks, building a savings fund for various projects, sponsoring home dances during high school, and organizing camping, hunting, and fishing adventures.

The two Templeton families have kept close ties over the years. John's three children—Jack, Anne, and Chris—have

spent several childhood summers in Winchester, staying with
Harvey and Jewel, and enjoying all kinds of activities with
their five children—Jill, Harvey, Handly, Avery, and Ann. During my visit, Jewel had great fun recounting some of the antics
of the kids, especially when they traveled with her to Florida
in Jewel's big black hearse, which she christened Queen Mary.

John and Harvey joined in, describing their travels with
their parents, including two winter vacations in Florida when
John was six and seven and two camping out motor trips,
which John's mother devised when John was fourteen and fifteen to visit the Northeast and California. Travel from Tennessee to Florida was something of an expedition in those
days; plans had to be laid carefully and preparations for the
unexpected had to be thorough. For their first Florida trip, in
1919, Vella wrote well ahead of time to Chicago for what was
called the *Blue Book.* In it were detailed directions for travel
throughout the country. Because there were virtually no road
signs on the 700-mile route from Chattanooga to St. Petersburg (part of the Dixie Highway from Chicago to Miami), a
guide book was of equal importance to the very essential
spare tubes, patches, and tire irons needed to keep the wheels
turning. There were no paved roads outside the few big cities.
And the part of the trip from Winchester to Chattanooga was
so hazardous that John's father and another man drove the
car to Chattanooga, a four-day trip of only seventy miles by
road and river barges while Vella and the two boys reached
Chattanooga by railroad. As the motor trip began, John's father and the two boys would sit in front, while John's mother
would sit in the back, reciting the directions from the *Blue
Book.* ("She was the original back-seat driver!" quipped John.)
The directions were fascinating in their detail, and made it
quite evident that the *Blue Book* had to be frequently updated.
John read the section for leaving Winchester:

> Once you leave Winchester you are on 7th and College Street
> at the far side of the Courthouse. Turn rt. on College St., go 0.1

mi., come to 4 corners, turn left, passing a school on the right, go another 0.1 mi., at end of road turn rt., cross the RR, then 0.7 mi. to a fork and bear rt. . . .

Sometimes the directions were less detailed, as in the following description of travel from Monteagle—farther along the road—to Jasper, a town close to Chattanooga.

Monteagle, 4 corners, station on the left, keep close along the RR, end of rd. turn rt., shortly descending Cumberland Mountains on a long easy grade. End of rd., turn left on macadam. Jasper courthouse on the left.

Besides getting lost, one had also to worry about getting stuck in the mud—which John said occurred about every hundred miles—and about finding places to sleep. But farmers along the well-traveled routes were quick to help with mules for towing for a fee and often allowed camping on their property overnight. Food was less of a problem, especially if you were as resourceful as the Templeton boys. John and Harvey often took turns perching on the running board of the moving car and shooting rabbits that had strayed onto the road!

All of this might seem a rather adventurous and risky undertaking for the parents of two small children, but it turns out to be perfectly consistent with the style of upbringing employed by Harvey and Vella Templeton. They gave the boys maximum freedom and every encouragement to try out new ideas and to design a variety of potentially useful projects, even if there were risks involved. Beginning with his butterfly collection, John was allowed to purchase cyanide from the local druggist, and soon after he was buying ammunition for his rifles and shotguns as well as gunpowder for fireworks displays. He and his brother were also extended unlimited credit in all the local stores, although John is quick to point out that they were careful to buy very little. John says of his early training:

> I can remember no time when my parents or teachers ever vol-
> unteered to me even one sentence of advice on ethics, religion,
> conduct, behavior, business, thrift, dress, hours, or homework.
> Of course my multitudes of questions as a child were an-
> swered thoughtfully; but after age twelve rarely did I ask.

John's performance in school continued to be exceptional. Valedictorian of his class at Central High School, he
also received four out of the five gold medals awarded—for
debate, public speaking, citizenship, and scholarship.

What John's parents and teachers gave him was a remarkable self-confidence, an assurance that he could realize high
goals and leave a mark on the world. One of his favorite poets,
first read in high school, is Henry Wadsworth Longfellow, and
he particularly likes several stanzas of "A Psalm of Life."

> . . . Tell me not, in mournful numbers,
>   Life is but an empty dream!
> For the soul is dead that slumbers,
>   And things are not what they seem.
> Life is real! Life is earnest!
>   And the grave is not its goal;
> Dust thou art, to dust returnest,
>   Was not spoken of the soul. . . .
>
> . . . Lives of great men all remind us
>   We can make our lives sublime,
> And, departing, leave behind us
>   Footprints on the sands of time.
>
> . . . Let us, then, be up and doing,
>   With a heart for any fate;
> Still achieving, still pursuing,
>   Learn to labor and to wait. . . .
>   "A Psalm of Life" (1839), St. 1, 2, 7, 9.

John's vision for his life began to take focus early in his
high school years.

> As a high school freshman, I decided to try to go to Yale, but
> this required taking examinations by the College Entrance

Examination Board, which no one from my high school had ever taken. From the board I bought copies of the old examinations for the four years past. Then each year when high school finished about May 20th, I began to study the subjects eight hours a day. Each year for three years I took the three-day College Entrance Board Examinations in Nashville the third week in June. Entrance to Yale required a minimum of four years of Latin, four years of English, and four years of mathematics. Central High School offered only three years of math, so the principal agreed to offer solid geometry and trigonometry as a fourth year class, provided I would teach the class and recruit at least eight friends so that the class would meet state requirements. The principal set the examinations for us, and graded them, and all of my students passed.

But the old saying about all work and no play making Jack a dull boy could not be said about the blossoming John Templeton. Upon entering high school he also discovered girls, and with the help of one pretty high school junior he learned to dance. Subsequently he began to invite a small group of students to his home for dances. John and Mary Mark Mowry, daughter of the president of the Farmer's National Bank, alternated locations—one weekend at Mowry's, the next at Templeton's. John also attended dances at the University of the South in Sewanee, and joined the Sigma Phi Omega fraternity at Sewanee Military Academy, preparatory to starting a chapter in Winchester.

Despite his mere 130 pounds, John also played on the Central High football team for three years. In a small school of fewer than two hundred it was not easy to find twenty-two boys who would commit the time to a rather demanding sport.

On the Road Again with John Templeton

The next morning, promptly at nine, Sir John and I embarked on another motor tour of Winchester. This time we traveled farther along on South High to the new cemetery, which John's brother had developed during his nursery days. There we saw the Templeton mausoleum. John's second wife, Irene Butler Templeton, who died in 1993, is buried there, along with her son Malcolm, who died suddenly in 1995. The inscription, "God is Love, and he who dwells in love, dwells in God and God in him," is taken from one of John and Irene's favorite passages from the New Testament (I John 4:16).

John and Irene and their families came together through the matchmaking efforts of John's son Christopher. John and his three children were living in Englewood, New Jersey, on the same street as Irene Butler and her two children. Four years earlier, John lost his wife Judith Dudley Folk through a tragic accident, and Irene was divorced.

> When my Christopher was six, I had been a widower four years. His favorite playmate was Malcolm, who lived with his sister and devoted mother Mrs. Irene Butler also on Chestnut Street in Englewood. One day, to Irene's great surprise, he phoned to ask if he could come to tea with her alone. After they drank tea together, Christopher said, "If you ever think of getting married again will you please consider my father?" Three years later Irene and I had a big church wedding in her St. Paul's Episcopal Church with all five of our children, ages eight to eighteen, as attendants. After our honeymoon at Jupiter Island Club, we all lived in my home and the Fisher's Island summer home with my Tennessee ladies, Rosezella Romney as governess and Mattie Whitworth as housekeeper.
>
> Irene and I wanted our five to feel more like one family, so we planned eight weeks driving all over Europe for the seven of us. We could not find in Europe an auto adequate for seven people plus luggage, so I bought a ten passenger Volkswagen bus. Thus we were able to invite my brother's three older children, Jill, Harvey III, and Handly. With no room for much luggage inside our bus, we bought a roof rack plus tarpaulin to keep the bags dry. All ten of us were limited to a single suitcase for eight weeks, including Irene, who often traveled before and after this trip with five or more.
>
> We knew our children were peculiar in the fact that each child wanted his own way. So we made each child the total

boss of some activity. John, Jr., aged eighteen, was the only one of the eight to have traveled in Europe so he was in charge of choosing cities and hotels. Although that July and August were the busiest Europe ever had, he wanted to make no reservations. Each day about five we would stop at a tea shop so he could have thirty minutes to get hotel rooms for the ten of us. To our great surprise, only thrice did he fail. In Frankfurt the best we could find was a former bomb shelter. Irene felt panic at the thought of not having windows but we all were good sports. When Jack could find no hotel in Ljubljana, in communist Slovenia, we all slept on cots in corridors of a high school. Jack found only a hay loft on Bank Holiday in Hemel Hempstead, England, but Irene charmed a male long distance phone operator who did find four rooms in a public house twenty miles away after ninety minutes of trying.

Jill, age eighteen, was boss of all finances and paid all bills and pocket money. Harvey, age seventeen, was boss of the timetable, maps, and guide books. Anne, age fifteen, was boss of mail and travel history and wrote five hundred words every other day about our adventure so my secretary in Englewood could make photocopies and mail them to all our friends. Wendy, age fifteen, was boss of everything relating to food. Handly, age fourteen, was boss of the bus and drivers. Malcolm, age nine, was camera man and took many pictures daily to mail to my secretary for distribution. Christopher, age ten, was famous for complaints, so he was in charge of "no grumbling." If any of the ten of us said anything negative, his job was to call us down. Before the complainer could continue, he or she had to say two pleasant things. After that only rarely did anyone want to continue his or her complaint.

Irene and I kept for ourselves only the hardest job, which was to keep our mouths shut while witnessing hundreds of childish mistakes. Each morning we would pack our single bag and sit on the back seat of the bus while the youngsters made all the usual mistakes about bills, maps, tips, etc. However, I made the only serious mistake. When I gave Jill $500 for expenses the first week, all the youngsters were excited by more money than they had ever seen in cash, so they asked what to do with a surplus any week they did not spend it all. I said I would be so pleased by such careful management that they could reward themselves by dividing the week's surplus among the eight. From that moment they would not let us rent a room with bath and we bought food at grocery stores. Handly decided his saving would be enough to buy his first used auto when he returned home. When I paid extra for Irene to have a room with bath during our two days climbing Gross Glockner mountain in Austria, all eight children lined up to use her bathtub.

At the end of the trip, we sold the bus for $100 more than we paid for it in Germany. Anne took the photos and her thirty adventure stories to make for each of us an illustrated history of the eight weeks, which welded our family together. My classmate at both Yale and Oxford, Arthur Gordon, was then an editor at *Cosmopolitan*. He wrote a great story of our adventure and sold it to *Good Housekeeping* for $1,500 and gave me half of that fee.

After John and I left the cemetery in Winchester, we drove across town to North High Street, to the site of the Handly house where John's mother was born. When Vella was a girl, her father sold the mill in Boiling Fork Creek and built a one-story home here on a half-block of land. Turning back into town, we passed the Cumberland Presbyterian Church, where the Handlys were long-term members. John's mother was a staunch supporter of this church, often cooking and serving dinners to various groups. Sometimes the church could not afford a minister, so services depended upon students from the School of Theology at the University of the South in nearby Sewanee. But Vella also earned enough money to pay half of the cost of supporting a missionary in China named Gam Sen Qua. Vella and her sister Leila also provided much of the leadership of the church, as the following letter from the daughter of one of the ministers attests:

Dear Mr. Templeton:
The article about you in the December 30, 1973 issue of the *Nashville Tennessean* brought back some wonderful memories.

Miss Vella and Miss Leila, as "women elders," were a new experience for my father, the Rev. W. B. Spraker, when he became their pastor at the Winchester Presbyterian Church in 1937. However, it did not take long for him to realize and appreciate their worth and faithfulness. Their prayers, coupled with their hard work, held that little church together for many years.

The garden Miss Vella grew to help you get to Yale also fed her pastor's family—as well as half the poor in Winchester. I wish I could tell you of the many happy memories I have of her. Her religion, pure and undefiled, has had a tremendous influence on my life.

This I am sure of . . . Miss Vella would be enormously proud of your success but not at all surprised at it nor at the fine person the article portrays you as having become.

My very best wishes for your continued usefulness and happiness.

Sincerely,
Alma Spraker

John's mother also got him involved at Cumberland. At the age of fifteen he was elected Sunday School superintendent, though he felt a bit uneasy about the post. As he expresses it: "This caused me to begin to develop some conscience, because I felt badly standing in front of all these good people knowing that I was not a very good Christian myself. . . . My thoughts were too often about girls, sports, and possessions."

Vella also introduced her family to the writings of Lowell Filmore through the Unity School of Christianity, then a new movement centered in Kansas City. Unity teaching stressed the power of faith and the potential of the individual, both of which have been powerful influences in John Templeton's life. To understand John's parents' hands-off attitude, one must first understand that Vella's faith included the belief that God can do what we can't if we give freedom and encouragement to our families and communities. Ideals of thrift and discipline and self-sufficiency therefore came to John early in childhood, yet were always tempered by a sense that all we had came from God, so should be accepted with humility and thankfulness.

One aspect of humility was reflected in the way Vella dressed her two young boys. Only on Sunday did John wear good clothes. The rest of the week the two youngsters wandered around town in overalls. When it was warm they went barefoot. On at least one occasion this lead to some embarrassment. When a government social worker came to town to evaluate the needs of the poor in the community, she and Vella happened to meet in the town drug store, and discussed how to clean up the poor children. To illustrate the need she pointed out the window at two small boys in overalls and bare feet. To Vella's embarrassment they were John and his brother Harvey. One sometimes pays a price for humility!

Riding back to Harvey and Jewel's for a second afternoon and dinner, I thought again about some of the other advantages John had had growing up in Winchester, Tennessee in the teens and twenties of this century. This was "small-town America." No one locked their doors. Motion pictures were wholesome. Television did not yet exist. There was essentially no drug problem and until 1933, when prohibition was repealed, there was little drinking of alcoholic beverages. On a personal level, John's mother was a leader in the local chapter of the Women's Christian Temperance Union, and John's father offered a reward of twenty dollars for the arrest of anyone with a whiskey still.

But perhaps the most significant thing—maybe still true in some parts of "small-town America"—is that phenomenon so rare in the business world ... trust. John Templeton learned the importance of trust from his parents and from an utterly powerful and trustworthy God, and used it as a powerful testimony in the investment world of our day.

CHAPTER 9

Reaching Out: Yale, Oxford, and Across the World

When John graduated as top scholar from central High School in Winchester, Tennessee in 1930, the world of economics and business was just beginning a long-strangling depression, which followed the stock market crash of 1929. But part of the tuition for his first year at Yale had already been set aside through a systematic savings plan devised by John's parents during the first world war. As John explains, "In the first world war citizens were asked to invest five dollars daily in war bonds, so my parents offered to give my brother and me (aged eight and five) each a dollar to put in ten-year bonds every day during the war when we did not fight with each other. Ten years later we used this to help with college tuition."

Because these savings were modest, John embarked on an ambitious plan to sell magazine subscriptions door to door. After responding to an advertisement in a magazine, he became one of a group of seven teenage boys who were driven from town to town by an employee-trainer of the Hearst Publishing Company. Their magazines were popular ones, *Good Housekeeping* and *Cosmopolitan,* and each subscription cost two dollars for the year. But most housewives were careful with their money in those hard times, and so a bargain was struck between Hearst Publishing and the boys. If each boy sold two hundred subscriptions in eight weeks, the publisher would pay room, board, and transport for the eight weeks and send two hundred dollars toward college tuition. Not only was this an almost impossible goal from an economic standpoint, it was also a forceful sales approach that John found distasteful. As he put it, it was "against my nature." For example, their trainer actually required them to run from house to house so that they would be breathless and so seem excited and forceful in their sales pitch. John guesses that perhaps a quarter of the housewives didn't even know what they had bought; only that some poor college student needed their help! John was one of only four boys who finished out the eight weeks and sold at least two hundred subscriptions. The income was only about 5 percent of what he needed for college, but the experience taught him special lessons about hard work and self-confidence. His brother Harvey jokes that the eight weeks had warped John's "southern gentleman" personality. Actually, John Templeton seems not to have lost any of his southern charm; he has been soft-spoken and gracious throughout his life. What those eight weeks really contributed, he says, was an important lesson in the perseverance needed for the trials of life.

John's first year at Yale was a new challenge, making new friends and settling down to work for a degree in economics. He had never been to New England and he encountered a new kind of elitism; two-thirds of Yale's 825 freshmen had attended private schools in the east in preparation for Ivy League colleges. This meant that many of them had friends in their class and in the upper classes as well. Because of this, John says, no public high school graduates were invited to join a fraternity. He is quick to disclaim that discrimination was involved, and actually, the next year he and various public high school graduates were invited.

Sophomore year at Yale was a very challenging one, with the economic crisis deepening all over the country. Back in Winchester, John's father was beginning to feel the pinch as a landlord and landowner, and that summer he announced that he would not be able to provide any tuition for Yale for the

The dedication of the Templeton Hall of the Princeton Theological Seminary, 1990. (*l to r*): Dr. Thomas Gillespie, president; John Marks Templeton, former chairman; Mrs. Irene Templeton; Dr. David Watermulder, chairman.

Templeton Hall of the Princeton Theological Seminary, 1990.

On the occasion of Sir John Templeton's election as an Honorary Fellow of Templeton College, Oxford. *Seated:* Sir John Templeton, Lady Irene Templeton, U. Kitzinger. *Middle row:* I. Kessler, B. Prodhan, E. Howard, S. Dopson, R. Undy, S. Jennings, R. Martin. *Back row:* R. Davies, J. McGee, C. Cowton, P. Anand, G. Fitzgerald, J. Purcell, J. Reynolds, R. Stewart, K. Blois.

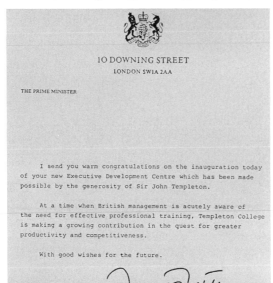

10 DOWNING STREET
LONDON SW1A 2AA

THE PRIME MINISTER

I send you warm congratulations on the inauguration today of your new Executive Development Centre which has been made possible by the generosity of Sir John Templeton.

At a time when British management is acutely aware of the need for effective professional training, Templeton College is making a growing contribution in the quest for greater productivity and competitiveness.

With good wishes for the future.

Margaret Thatcher

Letter from Margaret Thatcher recognizing the establishment of Templeton School of Management at Oxford University.

The Templeton Prize for Progress in Religion was awarded to Dr. Billy Graham in 1982. (*l to r*): John Marks Templeton, Mrs. Billy Graham, Dr. Billy Graham, HRH Prince Philip.

The plaque with three gold medallions bestowing knighthood on John Marks Templeton.

Sir John and Lady Templeton
leaving knighthood ceremony
at Buckingham Palace, 1989.

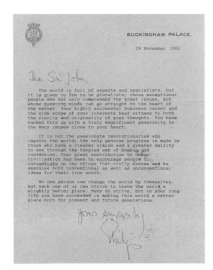

In 1992, Sir John was honored with
a festschrift, a collection of articles
by some of his most respected
friends and colleagues, which included this foreword written by
HRH Prince Philip.

The Templeton Window, donated by Sir John, at Lady Chapel, Westminster Abbey, 1996.

Westminster Abbey, London, where Sir John served on HRH Prince Philip's Restoration Commission, 1996.

John M. Templeton, Jr.,
Anne Templeton Zimmer-
man, and Christopher W.
Templeton in Casper,
Wyoming, 1990.

Dr. Anne Templeton Zim-
merman and Dr. Gail Zim-
merman on their wedding
day in Tucson, Arizona,
1979.

Drs. Jack and Pina Templeton and their daughters, Heather (*left*) and Jennifer, 1996.

Front row (*l to r*): Rhonda Zimmerman, Anne Zimmerman, Gail Zimmerman, Heather Templeton, Jennifer Templeton, Lady Templeton, Virginia and Susan Judith Templeton, Pina Templeton. *Back row* (*l to r*): Mike Zimmerman, Eva Zimmerman, Renee Zimmerman, Sir John Templeton, Jack Templeton, Christopher Templeton, Gäbriel Flynn, Jason Flynn.

Sir John Templeton with his son Christopher's daughter, Susan Judith.

Sir John and Lady Templeton, Mr. and Mrs. Harvey Templeton, Jr., and descendants in Winchester, Tennessee, 1992.

coming year. But as before, John responded with his unique form of resourcefulness and self-confidence. As he tells the story:

At the beginning of sophomore year (which was two years after the great stock market crash of 1929) my father told me with regret that he could not contribute even one dollar more to my education. At first this seemed to be a tragedy; but now looking back, it was the best thing that could have happened. It caused me to begin studying really hard to get top grades and thereby maintain two scholarships to help with the expenses. Mother had saved a little cash from selling vegetables and eggs, and I borrowed two hundred dollars from my Uncle Watson, which Mother paid back years later. This enabled me to travel to New Haven and to apply to the very well organized Yale Bureau of Student Employment, which was run by a capable man named Ogden Miller, who later became headmaster of the Gunnery School. He helped me to get scholarships and also to earn money at various jobs, such as being Senior Aide of Pierson College and chairman of the *Yale Banner and Pot Pourri* yearbook.

During these Great Depression years, one bank in which I had an account, the Broadway Bank, failed. Friends in New Haven said the safest bank in which to open a new account was the Mechanics Bank. About six months later, when walking by that bank, I saw a long line of people extending half a block from the front door. In those days this meant that there was a "run on the bank" and, of course, no one could get near enough to the cashiers' windows to withdraw money. Economics textbooks at that time said that savings depositors in Connecticut were paid off in bankruptcies at two dollars for each dollar paid to checking account depositors. Accordingly, I went to the savings deposit window where there was no one and opened an account by transferring to savings my entire checking account.

Although Yale was known as a rich boy's college, there was no discrimination of any kind against those of us working our way through. In fact, in those depression years, 42 percent of the students were earning at least part of their expenses. By hard study, I became the top scholar in the class by the end of junior year, which was helpful in being elected president of Phi Beta Kappa. This, in turn, was a great help toward selection for a Rhodes scholarship. I was tapped for the Yale Senior Society called Elihu and served as assistant business manager of the comic magazine called the *Yale Record*. When majoring in economics in 1932, I chose investment counsel as a profession because of deep interest in the difficulty in judging the true value of any shares of corporations. As a senior at Yale I earned one thousand dollars as the first Senior Aide of Pierson College. That was a tremendous help because it covered one-half of all that year's expenses. When the 1934 accounting for the Yale yearbook was finished, about eight hundred dollars in profit was distributed to me as chairman and used to open an account with my roommate, Jack Greene. He was then senior partner of a stock brokerage firm in Dayton, Ohio called Greene and Ladd because his father had died during Jack's junior year at Yale. This account is now forty-two years old but the name of the firm has changed to Cowen & Company. My first purchase of any stock was the seven dollar preferred stock of Standard Gas and Electric Company, which was selling at 12 percent of par because of the Great Depression. From that original eight hundred dollars and later savings have grown all of the investments I now own."

John's years at Yale would have to be characterized as tremendously energetic and full of enterprise. He readily admits that he was relieved when his excellent grades qualified him for scholarship money. After all the pressure and uncertainty of Yale, Oxford with expenses paid by Rhodes would seem like a bed of roses.

Oxford as a Rhodes Scholar

As Senior Aide at Pierson College at Yale, John guided students who were earning their tuition. In this capacity, and because he was top scholar at Yale as a junior, he was encouraged by Alan Valentine, master of Pierson College, and a member of the Rhodes Connecticut Selection Committee, to compete for a Rhodes scholarship. Only two students from each of the six New England states were allowed to compete for the four New England scholarships. John was one of those selected. After the interviews, the group had six hours to wait for the results, so John and Bob Michellet, an applicant from Dartmouth, decided to go to nearby Wellesley College. Surprisingly, they discovered that they both wanted to visit the same girl, Judith Dudley Folk of Nashville. Bob wanted to visit the girl recently voted the "most dated" girl in the Wellesley class of 1934, and John wanted to visit the girl who had been his sweetheart for two summers while she was staying at her family's summer home at Monteagle Sunday School Assembly Grounds in the mountains not far from Winchester, Tennessee. John and Judith were secretly engaged the next summer, and married three years later.

The sad part of the story is that Bob Michellet, who John would have invited to be a groomsman at the wedding, had died heroically while trying to rescue boys from a burning Dartmouth fraternity house, and the Rhodes scholars that year were one scholar short.

On arriving in Oxford, the Americans found a very different kind of academic setting; compared to the hectic pace of Yale, Oxford seemed like a rest period. The Rhodes scholarship was sufficiently generous that it was not necessary to work, which was fortunate because it was not considered proper for Oxford students to work for money. In fact, John says that at that time it was beneath the dignity of a student even to carry a parcel home from the store! At Oxford there were no grades and no examinations, and no classes to attend for two years until the formal examinations. Instead, instruction was by tutorial, and in John's case, this involved meeting one hour each week with a Mr. Tyler, a brilliant legal scholar of Balliol College. The choice was made for a program leading to a Bachelor of Arts degree because there was no program available in the study of business and certainly nothing on investments.

Many years later, John Templeton returned to Oxford to found Templeton College as the first college of the university devoted to postgraduate management studies. The beginnings of this institution date back to 1965, when the Oxford Centre for Management Studies was established in Kennington, Oxford, about a mile from the town center. In 1982, John was approached by Dr. Uwe Kitzinger, later to become president of Templeton College, and asked to become founder of what was to be the first Rhodes Scholar college at Oxford. John agreed, but with several important stipulations, which display his keen foresight and investment prowess. Dr. Kitzinger wrote in *The American Oxonian* in its Winter 1987 issue:

> John Templeton was interested in making a partnership contribution—keeping us on our toes and encouraging us still to find other benefactors—rather than supplying the totality of our needs. We were talking about a gift of $5 million and suggested re-naming ourselves in memory of his mother and father, Harvey and Vella Templeton. But the Fellows of the Centre and John Templeton thought it wise to follow through the thought expressed in the *American Oxonian* article and call it, in the future, a College. The governing Council of Management (on which the business community is strongly represented) after serious consideration, agreed: and in 1984 the University gave us the right to matriculate up to twelve postgraduate students in management each year.
>
> It quickly became clear that John Templeton was actively interested in what that College could actually do to advance management studies at the University, revitalise the British economy, and help people the world over manage their affairs better and escape from poverty, famine, and disease. And these concerns were urgent. He therefore made it explicit in the deed of gift that the money was not only to be spent rather than hoarded (the parable of the talents is one dear to his heart), but also that it was to be spent "effectively and expeditiously."
>
> Instead of handing over this gift to a Board of Trustees for long-term investment in farms or in stock market securities, and then only using the income derived from them, we were to invest it as working capital in ourselves—thus not just

gaining for management education the net profit from others' corporate operations, but increasing the volume of management education by the whole extent of our own additional turnover. The deed of gift shows how widely John Templeton interprets the concept of working capital: It includes quite explicitly not only such physical investments as buildings and equipment, but also such academic investment as funds to enable Fellows to use their sabbaticals to best advantage, such commercial investment as public relations, and such institutional investment as further fund-raising.

The Templeton deed also has another, closely related innovative feature: the "roll-over principle." There is always the temptation to devote unrestricted funds not to the most urgent purposes, but to those for which it would be most difficult to find specific donations. To free us from that concern, the trust deed therefore expressly allows us to use the gift in whatever is the most effective way for the realisation of its ultimate purposes: if later we find another donor to fund any particular investment already being financed by the Templeton benefaction, we are always still able to accept another gift, and name that particular item of investment—be it a student hall of residence or an executive centre or a new institute or fellowship—according to the next donor's wishes. The original funds are then rolled back into the Templeton benefaction to be used for the next most urgent purpose.

Templeton College was dedicated as a college of Oxford University in October 1984, in a ceremony attended by Keith Joseph, Britain's minister of education, and Lord Jenkins, the chancellor of the university. My wife and I were fortunate to be in attendance, and I remember that amid the various speeches, John Templeton's stood out, both for its remembrance of his parents, for whom the new college was dedicated, and for Sir John's characteristically public thanks to God for the manifold blessings we have all received. It raised some eyebrows, but I thought it was the high point of the ceremonies.

Because Oxford gave six weeks holiday at Christmas, six weeks at Easter, and fourteen weeks in the summer, John and his fellow Rhodes scholars had the time and good fortune to meet some fine English people and to explore the historic and artistic sights of Europe in a way few tourists would. The contacts with English society were arranged by Lady Francis Rider, who had initiated a program during World War I to introduce young American officers stationed in England to the best of English society. When the war was over, she arranged with the Cecil Rhodes Trust to invite Rhodes scholars to participate, and each year, at a tea party at Rhodes House in Oxford, the new scholars were invited to select families and dates and places they would like to visit. Among the possibilities were families with country homes and horses and others with castles by the sea, and the stay could be for a day or a weekend or for as long as two weeks. Formal invitations were mailed shortly thereafter, and included clothing suggestions—dinner jackets or formal white tie and tails, morning suits for some city homes. According to John, these visits were exciting and sometimes embarrassing, but always tremendous learning experiences.

The second kind of learning involved a series of well-planned trips, taking advantage of used copies of *Baedeker's* guide books for each of the European countries. John and his colleagues would study the guides thoroughly, then buy student railway tickets for unlimited mileage. They also took advantage of information supplied by the guide books about places to stay—inexpensive hotels, youth hostels, and YMCAs. These intensive learning experiences were achieved at very little expense and so were doubly satisfying to John, who carried his ideal of thrift well beyond the confines of Winchester and Yale.

In fact, John's thriftiness enabled him to save four hundred dollars while at Oxford, and to persuade a former Yale classmate, James Inksetter, who was studying at Cambridge, to join him in a seven-month trip through thirty-five countries after graduation from Oxford. As for thrift, John's expenses for that trip were an incredibly low ninety pounds. Hotels averaged only twenty-five cents per night, and by living at the poverty level, John and James learned much about the life of the masses in the rest of the world. The decision to make this never-to-be-forgotten trip was not made lightly. The years at Oxford had only served to reinforce John's decision to become an investment counselor, and he was already preparing for the job he wanted when he returned to America. Before leaving on the trip, he wrote a letter of introduction, setting forth his qualifications and goals, and mailed it to one hundred American brokers and investment advisers, asking for appointments when he returned from the trip. Furthermore, the trip itself was made with an eye to future investment opportunities, and given the international success of John's later investments, these seven months may have been the most educational period of his entire career!

Preparation for the trip also included decisions about how much they would carry, and how it could be protected. James Inksetter took a knapsack and John hired a seamstress to sew an over-the-shoulder roll like the one his grandfather, Dr. Robert Clinton Handly, carried in 1860 as a Confederate army surgeon. One side of the roll was a sleeping bag and the other side held one shirt, underwear, socks, rain coat, four *Baedeker* guide books, and a Bible. To reduce the risk of robbery, they used 80 percent of their money to buy traveler's checks, which they mailed ahead to American Express offices in Athens, Jerusalem, Hong Kong, and Tokyo.

The trip began with travel through northern Europe, and included a six-day stop at the 1936 Olympic Games in Berlin. There each morning the stadium resounded with "Seig Heil!" for fifteen minutes as the Nazi party demonstrated its allegiance to Adolph Hitler. From Germany, the two traveled through Hungary and Austria, then via boat on the Danube through Yugoslavia and Romania, then by third class rail through Bulgaria, and then by coastal boat to Greece. At each of the cities where John and James planned to stay overnight, they discovered that porters wearing caps advertising inexpensive hotels could be bargained with at the train stations. In this way, despite the language barrier, they were able to find fairly reasonable places to stay at very low cost. The least they paid for a bed was ten cents in Changsha, China, but the bed was made of wooden boards and the pillow a wooden block. "At least they were very clean!" John said.

Such was not the case in Bucharest, Romania, where an unfortunate mishap landed them in jail. Their problems began when they misread the train schedule, thinking the daily train to Varna, Bulgaria, left at 10 P.M. rather than 10 A.M. They had carefully spent all their Romanian money before walking to the station, so they crossed the street to sleep in the park for the night. Unfortunately, their choice of outdoor "hotel" made them look more like vagrants than anything else. In a few hours the local police appeared and asked them what they were doing in a language the two men couldn't understand. Eventually, they were hauled away to the police station, where they spent the rest of the night in a flea-infested cell. When they awoke the next morning, thousands of fleas were crawling over them, and they seemed to have at least as many flea bites. Some people might have given up at that point and gone home, but not these two adventurers. After picking the fleas off each other as thoroughly as they could, they left for Varna a little the worse for wear.

The most exciting and perilous part of their investment tour occurred in the Middle East, where John had a close brush with death and almost precipitated an international crisis. John recalls the experience:

> After diligent study of the antiquities, history, museums, economy, and people along the Nile, we bought third class bus tickets for the trip across the desert to Jerusalem. The British were then protecting the [area], so the bus was protected by an armored car. From the Bible we read carefully every mention of the disciples James and John and then tried to visit each location where they are mentioned and do what they did. In each letter to my mother, I tabulated the chapter and verse so she

could read what James and I were now doing daily. James and John were called by Jesus when they were fishermen on the Sea of Galilee, so we found a Jewish boy who spoke English and Arabic, who, in turn, found for us two Arab fishermen from the Golon Heights who agreed to help us catch a fish. The innkeeper told James this was dangerous, but I went boldly back to their row boat.

I took an oar to help the two fishermen row, but by sign language they insisted I sit on a pillow in the prow. I thought we could catch a fish in half an hour and be home before dark. But they rowed for three hours from Tiberius to the Golon Heights and then took me to their family's home, a tent of burlap for shade from the hot sun and a row of carpets inside covering the desert floor. Their mother ground a few coffee beans in a shallow cup with a spoonful of water and handed it to me. I drank it, although I do not normally drink coffee. That was a mistake because the mother had to start over with another saucer handed around the family circle and then to me for each of us to take a taste. This was a life-saver because it apparently meant that the family was giving me its protection. Soon great shouting started on the shore from a group of fishermen who had been mending nets. Brandishing long knives, they came toward us, apparently having decided I was either Jewish or English and therefore should die.

With tremendous shouting and wrestling the men from my tent held them back until another boy who spoke English could be found; meanwhile, I prayed. Fortunately, I carried my American passport and with that the boy persuaded them to return to mending their nets peacefully.

The row boat was pushed about fifty yards offshore and by sign language the men told me to sleep on the pillow. Because of the excitable fishermen on shore, I did not sleep but prayed until they thought they were waking me two hours before dawn. After rowing a mile offshore they put their net in the sea in a great horseshoe shape with us at the mouth. They then asked me to make maximum noise with the tin pan from which we had all eaten mush by hand the night before while they pounded on the boat sides to scare the fish who ran into the net, whose holes were just large enough that the larger fish heads could go through but then the gills kept them trapped. By pulling in the net we caught twenty-three good-sized St. Peter's fish of about two pounds each. Then by rowing two hours we returned to the spot we had started from. They insisted I keep the largest fish and I bought several packs of cigarettes to give each fisherman. With great smiling and bowing, they said goodbye and I then returned to the little inn where James and the inn keeper were overjoyed to see me.

John says that his mother had a premonition of his brush with death, and her dream had been so vivid that she literally gave him up for dead. Perhaps she could read between the lines of his daily letters and realized how explosive the situation was in Palestine.

The rest of the trip took John and James through India, China, and Japan. Here again they were able to meet the people and gauge their attitudes and lifestyles in a way that traveling first class would not have allowed. John came away with a better grasp of the grass-roots economies and practical political systems of a wide variety of nations. It would have a major impact on his pioneering decision to search the world for investment opportunities. Returning home, the two travelers told their story to a classmate, Arthur Gordon, who wrote an article about their adventure and sold it to *Good Housekeeping* magazine. Arthur shared the proceeds with John and James, which in turn paid half of the cost of their seven-month trip.

Marriage to Judith Dudley Folk

When John returned from his around-the-world trip in the spring of 1937, plans for his marriage to Judith Dudley Folk were well under way. The wedding was to be a major event in Nashville society, and the local society pages were full of pictures and stories of the garden parties and white tie dinners and dances that occurred over a period of perhaps ten days as the wedding party assembled. John and Dudley were married by the Episcopal bishop of Tennessee on April 17 with a reception following at Belle Meade Country Club. There were twelve bridesmaids and sixteen groomsmen and ushers, including many of John's friends from Yale and Oxford. John borrowed his mother's Pontiac, and he and Dudley drove for their two-week honeymoon to the floating gardens of Xochimilco near Mexico City. In May the two went to New York to find jobs. Dudley found a job earning $150 a month at Young and Rubicam, an advertising agency in the Chrysler Building. John got a job, also at $150 a month, in the newly formed investment counsel division of Fenner and Beane in Wall Street.

At this point, the emphasis shifted sharply back to what for both John and Dudley were high priorities—saving for investment with the emphasis on thrift.

CHAPTER 10

The Growth Years

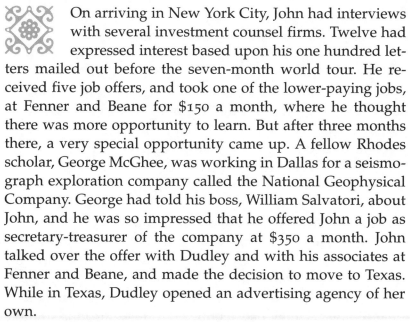 On arriving in New York City, John had interviews with several investment counsel firms. Twelve had expressed interest based upon his one hundred letters mailed out before the seven-month world tour. He received five job offers, and took one of the lower-paying jobs, at Fenner and Beane for $150 a month, where he thought there was more opportunity to learn. But after three months there, a very special opportunity came up. A fellow Rhodes scholar, George McGhee, was working in Dallas for a seismograph exploration company called the National Geophysical Company. George had told his boss, William Salvatori, about John, and he was so impressed that he offered John a job as secretary-treasurer of the company at $350 a month. John talked over the offer with Dudley and with his associates at Fenner and Beane, and made the decision to move to Texas. While in Texas, Dudley opened an advertising agency of her own.

John and Dudley had committed themselves to saving 50 percent of their incomes for investment, and so, when they returned to New York two years later, they were already in sight of the goal of an independent investment counseling firm. They continued to hold unflinchingly to the principle of thrift, and even made a game out of finding fantastic bargains in cars and houses and home furnishings.

Esmeralda and Other Bargains

John started bargain hunting early in life. When he was just twelve years old, he and some friends were playing in a hay barn about a mile from his house when he stumbled upon an old broken-down Ford. Seeing a potential bargain in the making, John asked the farmer who owned the barn if he would like to sell the car. The farmer replied that he would sell it for ten dollars, so John went home, withdrew some of his savings, explained the situation to his always agreeable mother, and bought the car. But now came the hard part—finding another Ford of the same model to use for spare parts to get the first one in working order. Finally, John located a matching Ford. If possible, it was in even worse condition than the first, but it had one virtue—it also only cost ten dollars.

With his equipment and parts assembled and tools borrowed from his brother Harvey, John and his eighth-grade friends moved to stage two of their plan—transferring the parts from one of the cars into the other. They were confident that they were smart enough to put a car together. If they got stuck in their effort to assemble a workable jalopy, they ran down to the local Ford dealer and pored over his repair manuals until they were clear on the principles to follow. They got to know the mechanics around Winchester and picked up valuable tips to help them complete their project.

After nearly half a year of working afternoons and weekends, John and his friends finally got one of the cars to run. They painted it orange and green and named it Esmeralda. And, surprisingly, with the help of constant and careful maintenance, the car they had rebuilt performed for four straight years, long enough to take the boys to and from classes and to play in out-of-town high school football games until they graduated from high school.

John, always aware of the importance of thrift, had recognized a bargain in those two cars and, with the help of his friends, had turned his dream into a reality, for only a twenty-dollar investment. As a matter of fact, the first five cars he owned were secondhand and none cost more than two hundred dollars. He never paid more for a car until his net worth exceeded one-quarter of a million dollars.

Thrift and bargain hunting went hand-in-hand in every aspect of John's life.

> Of course we paid all cash. We had been always scrupulous never to borrow. We paid all cash for autos and houses and everything else, so we would always be receivers and not pay-ers of interest. In 1941, after the first of our three children was born, we found a fifteen-year-old house in a good part of En-glewood, N.J. with three bedrooms, two baths, and two-thirds an acre of garden for $5,000 all cash, on the bus line within five miles of the George Washington Bridge to Manhattan. Five years later we were able to find a fifty-year-old twelve room home in the best residential area with one-and-a-half acres of garden for only $17,000 total all cash. Then we sold the $5,000 house for $17,000. Number 124 Chestnut Street was home until my partners and I sold our investment counsel companies to the Richardson family of North Carolina in 1959. Then we built our permanent home at the Lyford Cay Club in the Ba-hamas and began to build the Templeton Group of investment mutual funds.

Those twenty years during which he saved 50 percent of his income were not drudgery for John. In fact, he describes the early years in New York, when he and Dudley were set-ting up house, with great enthusiasm.

> To make thrift a joy rather than a burden, we made a game of it by telling our plan to all friends and relatives, who then gave us ideas. We found a furnished Manhattan apartment with a view of the East River for fifty dollars monthly. Our friends helped us find "blue plate" dinners in restaurants for 50 cents. In 1940, the only Manhattan apartment we could find for fifty dollars was on the sixth floor of a no-elevator building on East 88th Street. To furnish five rooms we could budget only

twenty-five dollars. Our friends watched newspapers for furniture auctions when people were moving away. At such auctions if anyone bid one dollar for a chair we said nothing, but if no one bid we said ten cents. Our costliest purchase was five dollars for a two hundred dollar sofa bed, which was so good we used it for twenty-five years. With such joyous games we furnished five rooms with mismatched furniture and carpets for twenty-five dollars.[2]

The Early Investment Years

In September of 1939, when Germany and Russia invaded Poland, it was obvious to John Templeton that a Second World War had begun. From his study of investment history, it also became clear that war was a time when even the least efficient businesses revive, because everything is in great demand regardless of price.

Accordingly, John decided to buy one hundred dollars worth of every stock on the stock exchanges that was selling for no more than a dollar per share. To finance this venture, he borrowed ten thousand dollars from his former boss, Dick Platt of Fenner and Beane, a somewhat unusual move for someone who ordinarily paid cash for everything. But this was borrowing of a different sort—borrowing money for a business venture in which the funds would be used to make money. John had great confidence that the stock market would behave as he predicted, with stock prices rising in the face of a wartime boom. Furthermore, John had the collateral to back up the loan; he and Dudley's personal investment portfolio was then worth more than thirty thousand dollars.

Dick Platt agreed to John's proposal although he remarked that 37 of the 104 companies in which John proposed to invest were currently in bankruptcy. John replied that he wanted all 104, whether or not in bankruptcy. It seemed a high risk move to Platt but, as it turned out, only 4 of the 104 companies became worthless. Within a year, John was able to pay back the money he had borrowed. After he had sold all the stocks, an average of four years after he bought them, the original ten thousand dollar investment had grown to more than forty thousand! John wished later that he had kept some of the stocks much longer, a lesson he put to good use with the Templeton Group of Investment Funds. John says of the 104 stocks:

> The best was the seven dollar preferred stock of Missouri Pacific Railway. When first issued investors paid one hundred dollars a share for seven dollars yearly preferred dividend. But in bankruptcy my one hundred dollars bought eight hundred shares. Gradually railways began achieving good earnings again. When up from one-eighth to five dollars a share, I felt grateful and sold out. Then within five years the price rose about $105 per share.

The idea of letting money work for you fascinated John Templeton. He would spend hours studying compound-interest tables and playing mental arithmetic games. He even figured out how much the Indians would have made if they had taken the twenty-four dollars in trinkets they had received in 1626 from the Dutch for Manhattan Island and invested it at 8 percent annual interest. According to his calculations, they would have had $255 billion by 1926, or about sixty times as much money as the U.S. Federal budget in that year. This meant they would have been able to buy all 14,000 acres of Manhattan back for $15 million per acre—and still have billions left over!

John's opportunity to launch his own investment counseling company came a year after he and Dudley had returned from Texas. He heard that an elderly man, George Towne, owned an investment counsel firm with only eight clients, and so he offered him five thousand dollars for his operation. The name was changed to Towne, Templeton and Dobbrow, and for the first time, John "had his name on the door." Two years later his firm merged with Vance, Chapin and Company and the name changed to Templeton, Dobbrow and Vance. John remembers that those years were lean ones in his investment world. At times the young firm could not earn enough to pay him any salary, so he was forced to rely on savings. However, his focus was on building a sound investment organization, and to make money for his investors. One of his top priorities was to build a research library, but the cost could be prohibitive. He heard that his old firm, Fenner and Beane, was merging with Merrill Lynch, and would no longer need its library. John offered twenty dollars for the research material and twelve bookcases, and his offer was accepted. Any one of the bookcases would have cost one hundred dollars new. John had caught his old company in the midst of a move when bargaining for unneeded books and furniture had no priority. A research library for twenty dollars. What a bargain!

John's habit of thrift pervaded his new investment firm. When he opened his investment counsel office in the RCA Building in New York's Rockefeller Center in 1940 he told his secretary never to buy a new typewriter. The value of typewriters declined 30 percent to 40 percent the day they leave the store. They bought reliable, secondhand machines, most of them no more than a few months old, for an average of 40 percent below retail price.

The typewriter principle, John reasoned, could be applied to office space. He didn't need to spend on show, on something glittery and new. He simply needed the right amount of room in which to function. When he found that he'd outgrown his space in the RCA Building, he decided that it would be more economical to have the research department near his home in Englewood, New Jersey. He found space in an old building above a drugstore, and because it was in disrepair, he was able to rent it for one dollar per square foot per year. Templeton spent a few hundred dollars fixing up the entrance to lend it an air of dignity. And, most important, he had more than two thousand square feet of office space for two thousand dollars a year.

Because of his devotion to thrift—in small items like typewriters as well as large ones like office space—John Templeton's corporation operated at a profit every year after the first two years.

John and Dudley's first child, John Jr., was born in New York City in 1939. Two years later, Anne Dudley was born, and five years after that, Christopher Winston, also in New York City, although the Templetons lived at that time in Englewood, New Jersey. They joined the First Presbyterian Church of Englewood, and John became involved in fund-raising and serving first as a deacon and later as an elder. At that time he also took on the chairmanship of the Board of Trustees of the YMCA of Bergen County. In 1940, he was elected to the Commission on Ecumenical Mission and Relations of the National Presbyterian Church and soon after as chairman of the managing committee for its $50 million endowment funds. Through meeting national church leaders, John was invited to many meetings of the General Assembly and the National Council of Churches and once as a guest at the World Council of Churches meeting in Geneva, Switzerland.

These were hectic years for the Templetons, with the investment corporation demanding more and more of John's time, just when he was involved with a growing family and with community activities. The only vacation John and Dudley had had since their honeymoon was a ten-day trip to Nassau in the Bahamas, while they still lived in Texas. John's business was going well; they had accumulated $150,000 by the time he bought Vance, Chapin and Company. So it seemed appropriate to take another vacation—this time in Bermuda. But then, just when everything seemed to be going just right, tragedy struck. In February 1951, Dudley was severely injured in a highway accident as she and John toured Bermuda on motorbikes. She had suffered severe internal head injuries and died in the hospital. Recently, their oldest son, John Jr., now a pediatric surgeon and trauma expert, told me that his mother was the victim of what was then a poorly understood type of injury, and that he too indirectly was the victim of trauma.

The three children were devastated by the sudden loss of their mother. John, of course, had not only the pain of her loss but the problem of going on. As he explained his predicament:

> I had three young children. I didn't know how to be a mother to them, but I had to try. I couldn't spend all day with them because I was in the midst of trying to build a business and earn a living. So I asked one of our two servants, Rosezella Romney, to become the governess for the children. After the first few weeks, I found that the best thing to do was to go back to work, to fill my mind with business. It was much better to keep my mind full of serving clients than to worry over what had happened.

The tragedy was doubly painful because it came just a few months after John's mother's death, in September of 1950. In less than a year, he had lost the two most important women in his life. Some people in such circumstances are bewildered if not embittered. But others, like John, are fortunate enough to have deep spiritual resources. Not only did he go back to investment counseling with vigor and determination, but he also accepted a position on the Board of Trustees of Princeton Theological Seminary, as a ministry to the church. Here he met gifted ministers with spiritual strength and insight, like Dr. Bryant Kirkland, then minister of the Fifth Avenue Presbyterian Church, and brilliant scholars like Dr. James McCord, who was president of the seminary for thirty years. Soon John became chairman of the seminary's endowment investment committee and served in that capacity for thirty-eight years. He also served as chairman of the trustees for twelve years. Princeton was a very important experience for John. Through interaction with Kirkland and McCord and other trustees, half of whom were ministers, John formulated much of his own plans for charity programs and foundations to emphasize the acquisition of new spiritual information through research.

Two other things happened in this same time period that also helped to ease the loss of Dudley. One was the purchase of a summer home on Fishers Island, New York, in Long Island Sound. There the three children spent each of the next six summers together, along with their governess and cook and sometimes a theology student who provided instruction in golf, tennis, swimming, and boating. John was away for most of these summer weeks, but flew in on the weekends. Incidentally, the house on Fishers Island was another bargain hunter's dream. Purchased at the time of a busy and threatening hurricane season, it cost $18,000 and was sold eventually by the children for $630,000. But John is quick to point out that real estate is not generally a good investment. It's "too individualistic," he says.

The other important event of that period was the initiation of a new business association, the Young Presidents Organization. John was invited to a luncheon at New York's Waldorf-Astoria by a stranger, Ray Hickock, president of Hickock Belt Company of Rochester, New York. After lunch, Hickcock said to his fifty guests that his father had died and left him in charge of the belt and leather company and, at the age of twenty-five, he felt the need to talk to other young executives about management issues and techniques. He asked if any of the young presidents in the room thought they could learn from each other at semi-annual conferences. Seventeen people raised their hands and put their names on a list for future meetings. John thought the story would end there, but Hickock had his public relations agent write a news story about the meeting for the *New York Times*. The response was overwhelming, with more than one hundred more young presidents wanting to be involved. Thus was born the Young

Presidents Organization, which grew to more than seven thousand members worldwide, with five-day meetings held twice yearly and with other special meetings on occasion.

At first, a prospective member had to have become president of a corporation before he reached the age of forty. At the same time, his company had to have a sales volume of at least $3 million a year or more than one hundred employees. While these last two criteria have changed over the years, the age requirement has remained the same.

Another qualification for membership was that you had to drop out when you reached age forty-nine. When John and some of his colleagues reached that age they decided they wanted to continue their friendships, so they formed an alumni organization called the Chief Executives Organization. All members were graduates of Y. P. O. and there was no upper age limit. Hoping to have conventions where they all knew each other and their spouses, they limited membership to one thousand. However, soon a duplicate group called the World Presidents Organization was formed; it too was open to every person who had been a member of Y. P. O. This organization eventually grew to be much larger than the Chief Executives Organization.

Making many new friends through Y. P. O. was a great tonic for John, not only for his business dealings but also in his social and spiritual life. Conversations often drifted easily from stocks and production quotas to personal subjects and even religious concepts. John said that these organizations were "marvelous ways to learn from each other how to be better presidents and share the joy of seeing old friends again." This would seem to be one of the hallmarks of John Templeton's approach to social life. Good friends, good conversation, but always with an eye to what is more worthwhile and life-changing . . . what is a good investment!

These, then, were the growth years, full of potent and challenging experiences for a wise, disciplined, and extremely energetic man. It was not illogical that they would lead to an extraordinary investment program called the Templeton Growth Fund Ltd., which John started in November, 1954. The achievements of this common stock mutual fund have been phenomenal. To illustrate, Leroy Paslay invested $100,000 Canadian at the beginning and with distributions reinvested, his family owned shares worth $37 million Canadian on April 30, 1996. This performance is believed to be the world's greatest mutual investment fund performance for that time period.

CHAPTER 11

Investing with John Templeton

The Templeton Investment Philosophy

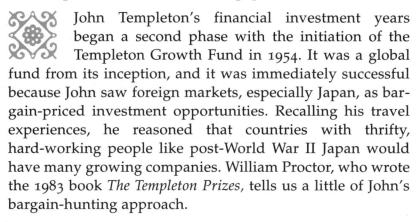 John Templeton's financial investment years began a second phase with the initiation of the Templeton Growth Fund in 1954. It was a global fund from its inception, and it was immediately successful because John saw foreign markets, especially Japan, as bargain-priced investment opportunities. Recalling his travel experiences, he reasoned that countries with thrifty, hard-working people like post-World War II Japan would have many growing companies. William Proctor, who wrote the 1983 book *The Templeton Prizes,* tells us a little of John's bargain-hunting approach.

> Templeton's basic formula is to divide the total value of a company by the number of shares the company has distributed. This calculation will give you the *true* value of a company's stock, and if the market price is lower, then it's a bargain. . . .
>
> At one point, for instance, Templeton decided that he liked the Yasuda Fire and Marine Insurance Company in Japan. He came to this conclusion after he took all the investments they owned, added up the listed market prices of those investments, and then divided this sum by the number of Yasuda shares outstanding. As a result, he discovered that the shares were priced 80 percent below their liquidating value. Now, that was a bargain, according to Templeton.

But many companies and other investment opportunities can't be evaluated in such a straightforward way. Like many savvy investors, if Templeton is evaluating retailing companies, for example, he looks to see the extent to which the geographical area is changing; the number and character of the people moving in and out of the vicinity; the nature of the company's competition; and the stability and competence of the management. And this is only the beginning. The more information Templeton collects about a specific company or industry, the better he is prepared, he feels, to make a final decision.

So he tends to fill all his "dead time"—the minutes and hours he spends on airplanes and buses, or waiting for appointments—with a sheaf of reports, graphs, and analyses on various companies and managers. He reads, studies, and weighs the pros and cons of each potential investment in light of these mountains of information. And then he decides. Only in this way can he have the confidence that he is using his personal gift of good judgment wisely, effectively, and accurately.

When Templeton is checking up on oil and gas companies, the wealth of information is still of prime importance. But the specifics are different from the specifics for a retail store chain. For oil and gas, he concentrates on the company's cash flow. Cash flow provides more reliable comparisons between oil producers because reported net profits are distorted by many arbitrary choices regarding accounting methods and exploration programs.

Each industry and company, then, has its own requirements when it comes to determining worth and bargains. When evaluating grocery chains, Templeton looks at net earnings. With mining companies he collects information on the ore bodies to estimate how long it will be before the minerals are depleted. The key point underlying his bargain-hunting methods is that his system of evaluating stocks is dependent on extensive research and sound judgment. There really is no easy formula that can be applied across the board to find a good investment value.[1]

John Templeton's keen analysis of investment opportunities gave him a significant edge over his competitors, but it also put a high priority on his time. As anyone who has handled many private accounts will tell you, the telephone never stops ringing. Each account represents a unique set of objectives and sensitivities to taxes, timing, and risk. Each client quite rightfully makes claims on a money manager's time. And for Templeton, time has always been a thing to be treated as a gift. Templeton's close associate John Galbraith says that:

> by nature, he doesn't want to waste time—so you don't ever find yourself sitting around exchanging small talk. You always have a sense that he has more things to do than time to do it. We noted that our meetings with him would always begin within a few minutes of the designated time, and always ended on schedule. Just as he respects his own time, Templeton extends that respect to the time of others. John Hunter, one of his Canadian stock brokers, says that when he tells him he will call at 9:15 Canadian time, the call will invariably come through at precisely that time—from wherever Templeton is traveling in the world. In fact, to ensure that he is prompt, he has always set his watch ten minutes fast.

Sir John's desire to use his time effectively and to help others through good money management found its logical expression in mutual funds—a means for "everyman" to stake a claim in the market. In a sense, he saw this field not only as a very good business, but as an opportunity to help families of many income levels save money and acquire wealth and security. A newspaper story covering a Templeton address to a Chicago financial group reported that among the stockbrokers and financial planners seeking his autograph was a young accountant who told Templeton "my daughter is two weeks old, and we just put $500 in your fund for her college education." Templeton shook his hand, saying, "we'll do our very best for you." He seemed genuinely concerned, and the man walked away with the satisfaction that his daughter's funds were in caring and capable hands.

The Principle of Maximum Pessimism

John Templeton is one of the most optimistic, up-beat people I have ever met. But he works in a world all but defeated by a dour pessimism, gripped by prophets of doom who have, like the newspapers and television news programs, almost always looked at the bad side. He does not deny that there is a bad side, but suggests that dwelling on good things leads to power, peace, and success whereas a focus on the negative leads to weakness, pain, and failure. However, he has used the prevalent negative tendency of others—especially investors—to forge a successful philosophy of investment. He calls it "the principle of maximum pessimism."

In 1978, John Templeton was featured on the cover of *Forbes* because the superb performance of the Templeton Growth Fund was then becoming well known through the marketing activities of his colleague John Galbraith. Just recently, John Templeton was again on the cover of *Forbes,* and the related article talked about his optimistic view of the world economy and how he used it in a counter-intuitive way to find the best investment bargains.

> When we last featured Templeton on our cover, in 1978, the Dow industrials were around 800, the economy was stagnating and some business publications were proclaiming the death of equities. Templeton's advice was unequivocal: Buy U.S. Stocks. They were then among the cheapest in the world. If U.S. Stocks did no more than get back to their traditional levels of around 14 times earnings, we would have a Dow of around 2800 by 1986. That's what he said. It sounded ridiculous at the time. Smart people were buying gold and collectibles and real estate, not stocks. Would stocks ever get that high again? "They always do," was Templeton's calm answer. And indeed they did.
>
> But it's 1995 and U.S. Stocks are no longer cheap by historical standards. On the other hand, the economy looks pretty strong. So, of course, we asked John Templeton: Where are the good buys now?

"People are always asking me where is the outlook good, but that's the wrong question," he responds. "The right question is: Where is the outlook the most miserable?" Templeton calls this approach to investing "the principle of maximum pessimism." Others might call it contrarianism. He explains it this way: "In almost every activity of normal life people try to go where the outlook is best. You look for a job in an industry with a good future, or build a factory where the prospects are best. But my contention is if you're selecting publicly traded investment, you have to do the opposite. You're trying to buy a share at the lowest possible price in relation to what that corporation is worth. And there's only one reason a share goes to a bargain price: Because other people are selling. There is no other reason. To get a bargain price, you've got to look for where the public is most frightened and pessimistic."[2]

John Templeton's optimistic expectations for the stock markets of the world have been thoroughly justified. Investment counselor Gary Moore, in his 1996 book *Ten Golden Rules for Financial Success*, quotes a *World Monitor* article of February 1993 in which John wrote:

> There will, of course, be corrections, perhaps even crashes. But over time our studies indicate stocks do go up—and up—and up. With the fall of communism and the sharply reduced threat of nuclear war, it appears that the U.S. and some form of an economically united Europe may be about to enter the most glorious period in their history. . . . Business is likely to boom. Wealth will increase. . . . By the time the 21st century begins—it's just around the corner, you know—I think there is at least an even chance that the Dow Jones Industrial Average may have reached 6000, perhaps more. Despite all the current gloom about the economy and about the future, more people will have more money than ever before in history.[3]

The Dow had reached 8,000 in 1997.

The Move to the Bahamas

Phase II of John Templeton's investment program ended in 1968 with his decision to move his permanent home to Lyford Cay on the Island of New Providence in the Bahamas. The 1960s were a time of spiritual renewal for John. He and Irene Butler had married in 1958, four years after he started the Growth Fund, and in 1959 he sold his New York investment counsel firm to an insurance company. John sought the move as an opportunity to devote more time to spiritual progress; as he put it, "I had spent my early career helping people improve their personal finances, but helping them to grow spiritually began to seem so much more important."

John and Irene built a beautiful home on a hill in Lyford Cay, overlooking a fine golf course and the Lyford Cay Club, a private club of 1,100 members from twenty-four countries. The native Bahamians are a people of deep spirituality and, in order to participate fully in this new country, then a British colony, he became a British citizen. He also began a program of spiritual training for Bahamians interested in the Christian ministry, providing a number of fellowships for study in the Bahamas and at Princeton Theological Seminary. Later he founded Templeton Theological Seminary, the first theological college in the Bahamas.

But John Templeton didn't shift completely away from financial investment management, since he still owned one mutual fund, the Templeton Growth Fund. As it turned out, the Growth Fund performance in the Bahamas was even better than before. John smiles as he recalls that his office was two rooms rented above a barber shop in the Lyford Cay Shopping Center at the start. Mena Griffiths, who is with him still, was his half-time secretary. It also turned out that Lyford Cay had other advantages. As he says:

> With the advantage of hindsight now, I think there are two reasons for this success. One is that if you're going to produce a better record than other people, you must not buy the same

things as the other people. If you're going to have a superior record, you have to do something different from what the other security analysts are doing. And when you're a thousand miles away from Wall Street in a different nation, it's easier to be independent and buy the things that other people are selling, and sell the things that other people are buying. So that independence has proved to be a valuable help in our long-range performance.

Then, the other factor is that so much of my time in New York was taken up with administration and in serving hundreds of clients that I didn't have the time for the study and research that are essential for a chartered financial analyst. And that was the area in which God had given me some talents. So now in the Bahamas I had more time to search for the best bargains.

Another very important aspect of John Templeton's continuing success in the investment world relates directly to his growing spiritual commitment. For instance, he never overlooks the importance of prayer.

We start all of our meetings, including our shareholders meetings and our directors meeting, with prayer. If you start meetings with prayer, the meetings are more fruitful and more productive—you reach decisions that are more likely to help everybody concerned. There is less controversy if you begin a meeting with prayer. Or, as I like to say, "Prayer helps you to think more clearly."

It goes back to my concept of God and His creative process. God is infinite. Maybe everything that exists in the universe and, much more, *beyond* the universe, *is* God. This means that the whole visible universe may be a small part of God and is itself a manifestation of God. By the word "manifest" I mean that which is able to be known by a human being. So one little piece of God has become known to us through light waves and other things that enable us to perceive a few features of the universe.

We ourselves seem to be a recent creation of God and a little part of God. If we realize this and try to bring ourselves into harmony with God, with the Infinite Spirit—if we try to be humble tools in God's hands and become clear channels for His purposes—then we can accomplish much more. And what we do accomplish may be more permanent and lasting.

Whatever you do in life—whether you get married, bring a case to a law court, operate on a child, or buy a stock—you should open with prayer. And that prayer should be that God will use you as a clear channel for His wisdom and His love. You should open with prayer that every thought in your mind and every word and action that is taken will be in tune with what is right in God's purposes, and for the benefit of all God's children and not just a selfish goal.

And if you pray this way, everything you do following such a prayer is likely to be more successful. Your mind is not twisted by conflicts. You're less likely to disagree with your associates or do something you'll regret next year. So your decision-making may be improved if you try to bring yourself into contact with the Creator, into harmony with His purposes.

If you make this basic effort to be in harmony with God and all of His children through prayer, then it's far more likely that anything you do in life will turn out for the best, including your selection of stocks. When we have directors or shareholders meetings or business meetings to discuss investment selections—whatever we do—we begin with prayer. We don't pray that a particular stock we bought yesterday will go up in price today, because that just doesn't work, but we do pray that the decisions we make today will be wise decisions and that our talks about different stocks will be wise talks. Of course, those decisions and discussions are not always wise—no one should expect that when he opens with prayer, every decision he makes is going to be profitable. Evidence shows that more of them are good if you open with prayer than if you don't.

Evidence also shows that John has been fair in his dealings with others. In more than sixty years in the corporate world, neither he nor any of the dozens of corporations controlled by him has ever sued or been sued. This may reflect Sir John's policy of ethics, peace, harmony, and love for everyone without exception.

The result of his merging of his spiritual and professional lives seems to have made both his efforts in the spiritual domain and his investment activities prosper. John set a schedule which divided his time equally between religious and philanthropic activities on the one hand and overseeing family investments and the mutual funds on the other. He had begun a program of double-tithing in the mid-1960s (in fact, John regularly gives to charity twenty times as much as he spends on himself) but now he was giving his time as well.

The Rise to International Prominence

John Galbraith joined John Templeton in 1974, at a time when the Growth Fund had reached $13 million in assets, but was, like all other mutual funds, in a market slump. It was Galbraith who brought the necessary marketing skills to bring the Templeton record of success to the wider public. The success of this combination was meteoric: in just four years the assets of the funds reached $100 million; when the funds' management corporation was finally sold in 1992 there were $22 billion in assets; and in 1997 the funds' assets had grown to the extent that more than 4 million people worldwide owned $80 billion.

In 1960, John Galbraith had been an accountant working in the earlier mutual funds managed by the investment counsel firm John Templeton had sold to the Richardson family. But in 1974 the Piedmont Company, as it was called, chose to move to the west, so Galbraith began looking for a new job. He approached John Templeton with a proposition to market the Templeton Growth Fund, setting up a U.S.-based network of brokers and dealers. His business plan was presented to John Templeton at Lyford Cay in that same year. Galbraith noted that the Growth Fund had only grown from $7 million to $13 million in assets during its first twenty years, despite its outstanding performance. The problem, he said, was marketing. He proposed to multiply the assets of the fund by tenfold in ten years. If he succeeded, Galbraith would buy the management of the fund, paying for it over the next three years. If he was unsuccessful John Templeton would keep it all. According to Galbraith, John responded, "Did you bring your swim trunks?!" Whereupon they went off to the Lyford Cay Club for a swim. As they sat on the beach, John said, "There are lots of people who want to buy my company, but I don't want to sell. Why don't you do everything you proposed, but buy 20 percent of my company? John Galbraith says he went home a bit disappointed, and told his wife Rosemary, "I went for the whole loaf and I got half." But then he quickly added, "What I thought was half a loaf turned out to be *many loaves*."

In 1978, John Templeton started a second fund, the Templeton World Fund, at John Galbraith's suggestion. In subsequent years additional mutual funds were introduced to focus on small companies and development of foreign nations. Stockholders meetings were held in a variety of locations, including the World Trade Center in New York, with the help of Galbraith's long-term associate Milton Steren, although the biggest meetings continued to be in Toronto. Seven thousand stockholders in five cities attended by TV the Toronto Annual Meeting in 1997. The Templeton Growth Fund in Canada has been a long-time success story, with strong leaders in accountant Bruce MacGowan, the first full-time employee in the Toronto office, and the new manager, Donald Reed. The Canadian Fund has a significant share of all mutual fund business in Canada. John Templeton has been an active presence at all the stockholders meetings, and he has encouraged his son, Jack Templeton, to participate as well. Despite Jack's demanding medical career, he has taken an active part in the meetings of the Templeton Funds. He has opened these meetings with prayer since 1985.

By 1978, John Templeton's investment work load had increased to such an extent that he hired Tom Hansberger, a Ft. Lauderdale, Florida, investment counselor, to assist him. They worked together, dividing the work between the Lyford Cay office and an office in Ft. Lauderdale. In 1985, John Templeton hired Mark Holowesko, a young Bahamian-born investment counselor. At twenty-five Mark was one of the youngest chartered financial analysts. In 1992 he became director and chief investment officer of Templeton Worldwide, Inc. In 1986 the two operations, John Templeton's in Lyford Cay and John Galbraith's (by then located in St. Petersburg, Florida), merged to become Templeton, Galbraith and Hansberger, Ltd.

In 1992 all management and marketing activities of the Templeton family of mutual funds was sold to Franklin Resources, Inc., a larger mutual fund manager in San Mateo, California. At that time, the many Templeton Funds had assets of $22 billion managed by some of the top talent in the field of investment. This helped Franklin Resources, Inc. to become one of the largest and most respected investment companies worldwide with offices in fourteen nations and more than five thousand employees.

Throughout this monumental phase of John Templeton's investment career, several salient features are evident. One is his frequent reference to common sense as a part of decision making. Time and again, says Bruce MacGowan of the Toronto office, John would respond in the question and answer period of stockholders meetings with the words, "it's just common sense," and then follow those words with a clear, concise but sensitive answer. One of John's long-term business friends, Burton Morgan, a fellow member of the Young Presidents Organization, recalls such an encounter at a YPO shipboard seminar titled "Mergers and Acquisitions." In the question and answer period, Morgan shared a major problem he was facing. He says of the encounter:

> I was number four to raise my hand. I said "I started this company, Fasson, and now own 15 percent of the stock. I originally bought 5 percent for cash and two options of 5 percent each, giving me the 15 percent. My total options would give me 25 percent, but my partner never meant to give me so much. I am an employee and stand to make a million dollars. He has asked me to give up the last two options, and I have refused. The only way he could not pay is to fire me because the

options are good only if I am employed. He will not buy my shares for fear I will start up again, so he has my money, and I have no job. What can I do?"

John replied, "Take your shares and go to an investment banker. With these shares as collateral, he will give you 25 percent of a new company and provide $500,000 in equity for his 75 percent. You can then borrow $500,000 from a bank and get a contractor to lease you a new plant."

"You mean I can really do this?"

"Certainly. Next!"

This gave me the courage to take what I had and to start Morgan Achesin from scratch. Before I met John, I had given up. I was out looking for an engineering job, and I felt that I would never again get a real entrepreneurial chance.

This was the single greatest boost of courage I have ever had and I have never forgotten John Templeton.[4]

John Galbraith, too, lauds John Templeton's performance at meetings with brokers and salesmen as well as stockholders. In fact, he arranged for Templeton to appear on the television program *Wall Street Week* with Louis Rukeyser in 1980. John has been on the program fourteen times since, more times than any other guest, and Louis refers to him as "one of the authentic heroes of Wall Street."

CHAPTER 12

John Templeton's Spiritual Investment Program

The Templeton Prize

 While the Templeton Mutual Funds were making headlines in the financial world, John was also busy in the spiritual domain. In 1972, he created the Templeton Prize for Progress in Religion, an annual cash gift exceeding in value the Nobel Prizes to honor individuals making a significant contribution to progress in religion. His first thoughts of a prize for religion stemmed from a recognition that many of his friends—especially the best-educated and most successful—seemed to be neglecting religion. He recalls that "they thought of religion as uninteresting and old-fashioned, or even obsolete."

In contrast, some of the work he was doing with religious organizations like the United Presbyterian Church Commission on Ecumenical Mission and Relations and the Princeton Theological Seminary called his attention to, in his words, "the marvelous new things going on in religion. There were new churches being formed; new schools of thought arising; new books being written on spiritual matters; new religious orders being established; and new denominations appearing. And I thought, how wonderful it would be if my friends could hear about these things and read about them. They couldn't help but be uplifted and inspired if they could just be informed about what was happening."

Then, too, the general tone of press coverage around the world seemed to ignore or even run counter to the religious movements that John Templeton was noticing. He says, "I struggled with this issue for a long time. Finally, I decided that, because I had limited resources and was just one person, the best I could do was to try to single out some of these wonderful people and help them to become more well-known—not so much for their own benefit, but for the benefit of people who might be inspired by them."

So, just as Alfred Nobel had done at the turn of the last century, John placed in his will a stipulation that, after his death, his trustees would award a prize for progress in Christianity. "But then I began to realize that it was a mistake for me to leave the assets for later use," he says, "because 'later' might be a long, long time away; I might live twenty years, and in that case the world and my living friends would miss out in hearing about these wonderful religious movements and people." So John sought advice from his long-term associate Dr. James McCord, the president of Princeton Theological Seminary, and also from Lord Thurlow, the former governor of the Bahamas. Both of them encouraged him to go ahead with the program of prizes while he was still alive. At the same time, John decided to broaden the religious base of the prize. He says, "It was during those formative years, particularly when talking with friends in the World Council of Churches, that we decided also that it would be a prize for progress in religion of all types, so no child of God would feel excluded." To confirm this idea, John convened a panel of nine prestigious judges, with at least one judge from each of the five major religions. In addition, at least half of the judges would be nonprofessionals in religion. "In this way," he said, "they would be more likely to be receptive to new ideas." John also set up an extensive system of nominators representing all the denominations of the Christian Church and several other religions. Lastly, John found a very distinguished person to award the prize. "In my early conversations with Lord Thurlow and Dr. James McCord, both of whom were selected to serve on our first board of judges, I said, 'If we had a really famous person to award the prize, it would be beneficial to a much larger number of people.' With the help of Lord Thurlow's friend, Sir Robin Woods, then Dean of Windsor, His Royal Highness Prince Philip, husband of the queen, graciously consented to award the first prize in 1973 and has continued to do so each year."

Some of those who have served as judges for the Templeton Prize include Presidents Gerald Ford and George Bush; Baroness Margaret Thatcher, former prime minister of Great Britain; the Dalai Lama of Tibet; Senators Orrin Hatch, a Mormon, and Mark Hatfield, an evangelical; Her Majesty Fabiola, Queen of the Belgians; Sir Mohammed Khan of Pakistan, former president of the International Court of Justice at the Hague; Lord Yehudi Menuhin, violinist from England; the Reverend Dr. Norman Vincent Peale, minister of New York's Marble Collegiate Church; the Reverend Dr. Arthur Peacocke, former dean of Clare College, Cambridge, and subsequently director of the Ian Ramsey Center, Oxford; and Princess Poon Pismai Diskul of Thailand, the former president of the World Federation of Buddhists.

The early recipients of the Templeton Prize, including Mother Teresa of Calcutta, the first recipient, in 1973, are ably described by William Proctor in his book, *The Templeton Prizes.* Since that book was published in 1983 there have been sixteen more winners, one each year except for 1989 and 1990 when two individuals shared the prize. The complete list of winners is included in Appendix D. Among this group of winners are several who have been leaders in the recognition of the impact of current science on theology. These include Sir Alister Hardy, who was knighted for his work in marine biology but who was also a leading researcher into the nature and extent of religious experience. Stanley Jaki, a Benedictine priest and a professor of astrophysics at Seton Hall University, has written several books about science, philosophy, and faith.

Professor Carl Friedrich von Weizsäcker of Starnberg, Germany received the award for his work on the relationship of physics and cosmology to theology. Professor Charles Birch, an Australian biochemist at the University of Sydney, has found process theology compatible with current science. The 1995 winner was mathematical physicist Professor Paul Davies of the University of Adelaide, who has written more than a dozen books revealing how physics, mathematics, and cosmology point to purpose and meaning in the universe.

Each occasion of recognition of the prize winner has been memorable, and I have been fortunate to have been present for the last five ceremonies. I especially remember the ceremony for Paul Davies, which I recalled in an article in *Progress in Theology.*

> On the third of May of 1995, Paul Davies became the twenty-fifth recipient of the Templeton Prize for Progress in Religion. The ceremony was held at London's Westminster Abbey, and in his acceptance speech, Professor Davies remarked that it was a special thrill to be standing just a few meters from the remains of Isaac Newton, one of the "great heroes" of his own discipline, physics.
>
> On this occasion it is appropriate to remark that many of us look at Paul Davies as a new kind of hero in physics, one who has opened the way to a new arena of dialogue in which scientists, philosophers, and theologians look at each other's disciplines with new respect and at their own discipline with a fresh kind of humility. For Paul Davies, that humble probing spirit has been evident throughout his many excellent books, of which some of the best-known are *God and the New Physics, The Cosmic Blueprint, The Mind of God, Other Worlds, About Time,* and *Are We Alone?*
>
> Paul Davies was born in London in 1946 and attended Woodhouse Grammar School in North Finchley. Later he attended University College, London, receiving a bachelor of science degree in 1967 and a Ph.D. in theoretical physics in 1970. After two years of postdoctoral research at Cambridge,

he spent the next eight years as lecturer at King's College, London, concentrating his research on the theory of quantum fields in curved space-time. In 1980 he became professor of theoretical physics at the University of Newcastle-upon-Tyne. In 1990 he moved to Australia to the University of Adelaide as chair of mathematical physics and three years later accepted a new position at Adelaide as professor of natural philosophy.

In his acceptance speech for the Templeton Prize, Paul Davies noted with great appreciation that one of the judges for the prize, Baroness Margaret Thatcher, had also been involved in an earlier award, when she, as a member of Parliament, had presented him as a schoolboy with a copy of *Norton's Star Atlas* for proficiency in his O level exams. He says it was a deciding point for him—the beginning of a long and exciting career in science.

Readers of his books also know that his career has gone well beyond that of most of his colleagues in probing the nature of the universe. What he has found is a universe that is unceasingly creative yet incredibly lawful. And he believes this discovery is of deep significance for both the scientist and the theologian. Of the scientific enterprise he has said "A lot of people are hostile to science because it demystifies nature. They prefer the mystery. They would rather live in ignorance of the way the world works and our place within it. For me, the beauty of science is *precisely* the demystification because it reveals just how truly wonderful the physical universe really is. It is impossible to be a scientist working at the frontier without being awed by the elegance, ingenuity, and harmony of the law-like order in nature.

"In my attempts to popularize science, I'm driven by the desire to share my own sense of excitement and awe with the wider community; I want to tell people the good news. The fact that we are able to do science, that we can comprehend the hidden laws of nature, I regard as a gift of immense significance. Science, properly conducted, is a wonderfully enriching and humanizing enterprise. I cannot believe that using this gift called science—using it wisely, of course—is wrong. It is good that we should know."

For the theologian, Paul Davies sees profound significance in the creativity and intelligibility of nature. At Westminster Abbey, he also said,

"Now some of my colleagues embrace the same scientific
facts as I, but deny any deeper significance. They shrug aside
the breathtaking ingenuity of the laws of physics, the extraordinary felicity of nature, and the surprising intelligibility of the
physical world, accepting these things as a package of marvels
that just happens to be.

"But I cannot do this. To me, the contrived nature of
physical existence is just too fantastic for me to take on board
as simply 'given.' It points forcefully to a deeper underlying
meaning to existence. The emergence of life and consciousness, I maintain, are written into the laws of the universe in a
very basic way."

Indeed, Paul Davies has become fascinated with the
quest for understanding how mind and matter are related.
Perhaps this second prize—the Templeton Prize—will make
him as fruitful in this search as did that first prize at Wood-
house Grammar School![1]

This occasion was a very special one for Sir John Templeton as well, for he has been a friend and encourager of Paul
Davies who, in turn, is an advisor to the Templeton Foundation.

Indeed, these have been exciting times for the goals of
the Templeton Prize, for as John Templeton realized so very
early, science is opening up a whole world of opportunity for
acquiring new spiritual information and hence for progress in
religion.

The Templeton Foundation

A second great step in John Templeton's spiritual journey was
made in 1987 when he established the John Templeton Foundation in Sewanee, Tennessee. Its primary purpose was to
explore and encourage the relationship between science and
religion, bringing together scientists, theologians, medical

professionals, philosophers, philanthropists, and other scholars to plan programs and help publish the tremendous opportunities for new spiritual information through research.

The first meetings of the Foundation were small. There
were the usual officers: John Templeton as chairman, his son
Dr. Jack Templeton as president, his niece Ann Templeton
Cameron as treasurer and his nephew Harvey M. Templeton
III as secretary. There were five trustees: Sir John, his wife
Lady Irene Butler Templeton, his son Jack, and two others,
Reverend Professor Thomas Torrance (Templeton prize-win-
ner of 1978), and myself (by virtue of my close working rela-
tionship to Sir John and by being executive director of the
American Scientific Affiliation, a 2,200-member organization
of Christians in science).

Recruitment of a staff for the organization began in the
following year, when Frances Schapperle, a former staff
member of the Robert Wood Johnson Foundation, became executive assistant. I first met Frances while I was doing some
writing and research at the Center of Theological Inquiry in
Princeton, New Jersey, in December of 1988. She wanted to
talk about the goals of the Templeton Foundation and about
Sir John, to get some idea of what it would be like to develop
a set of programs almost "out of whole cloth," and what it
would be like to work closely with a man known mostly as a
world-class investor but now becoming better known for
his philanthropic activities and especially for his interest in
progress in religion. I told her I thought the job would be challenging, not only because it would involve administering a
very new kind of program, which was virtually without
precedent, but also because John Templeton is a unique person who carries an enormous amount of information in his
head. It would be her job to put his ideas and the many projects he is involved in down on paper. Sir John was involved
in a great variety of philanthropic activities, especially in
North America and Europe, but to my knowledge only the
Templeton Prize had an administrator, Reverend Wilbert

Forker, assisted by Sir John's personal executive secretary, Mena Griffiths.

When Frances Schapperle came on board, she began to assemble a list of projects receiving support, which included the following:

- College Honor Roll for Character-Building Colleges;
- "Laws of Life" Essay Contest;
- Religious Editors Prize;
- Religious Heritage of America Awards Program;
- Templeton College, Oxford;
- Templeton United Kingdom Projects Trust; and
- Unity and the Association of Unity Churches.

The most time-honored is probably the Templeton United Kingdom Projects Trust, which has been administered by clergy at Windsor Castle since 1984. It has provided four awards yearly totaling £12,000 to honor British individuals and organizations that have made significant contributions to progress in religion in the United Kingdom.

Also included in Frances Schapperle's first annual report was a list of book projects under way, which included:

- *Who's Who in Theology and Science,* a directory of scholars in the science-religion field;
- *The God Who Would Be Known* by John Templeton and Robert Herrmann, published in 1989, and their second book, *Is God the Only Reality?*, eventually published in 1994;
- A "Laws of Life" textbook, which eventually became *Worldwide Laws of Life;*
- *Looking Forward: The Next Forty Years,* edited by John Templeton; and
- *Riches for the Mind and Spirit: John Marks Templeton's Treasury of Words to Help, Inspire and Live By*

One of the early activities of the Foundation was the production of a set of bylaws. Sir John was determined to describe his goals for the Foundation as clearly as possible, recognizing that many foundations have strayed from their original goals because the founder's wishes were not made sufficiently specific. I became involved in this process, helping John organize his ideas about a theology of humility into a major statement for the bylaws. John put down his ideas in a series of one-sentence statements, which were designed to raise the awareness of the infinite size and all-encompassing nature of God, of the dynamic nature of His activity and the incredible variety of His on-going creations, and of our response in humility as we recognize that we know almost nothing about this Unlimited Creative Spirit. These statements were then organized into paragraphs characterizing the theology of humility as:

- Centered in an Infinite God;
- Creative, progressive;
- Diversity.

Then followed a section outlining some potential benefits under the heading of "Encouraging Progress." John involved a number of associates in this process, including theologian and trustee Thomas Torrance. Professor Torrance's input was extremely helpful, but he had difficulty with the idea that man was a part of God, a salient point in Sir John's emphasis on the inseparability of God from all of creation. Professor Torrance left the Board the following year, but others were soon added, including Bryant Kirkland, with whom John had been associated at the American Bible Society and at Princeton Seminary, and Glenn Mosley, executive director of the Association of Unity Churches. Among later additions were Russell Stannard, professor of physics at the Open University in England, and William Simon, former secretary of the Treasury.

The annual board meeting was convened each year, in early June in Sewanee or Monteagle, Tennessee. The meetings were large because all the family, as members of the Foundation, were invited to the members' meeting which preceded the trustees' meeting. Here the purposes of the Foundation and its various programs were described by Sir John. Several family members were involved in programs, including Becky and Handly Templeton, who pioneered the first "Laws of Life" essay contest in the Franklin County Schools. Also present, besides Lady Irene Templeton, were Harvey and Jewel Templeton, John's brother and sister-in-law. Jack Templeton was of course there as member, trustee, and president, and he was often accompanied by his spouse, Dr. Josephine Templeton, an anesthesiologist, and sometimes by their daughters Heather and Jennifer. John's daughter, Dr. Anne Zimmerman, like Jack, also a surgeon, attended with her spouse Dr. Gail Zimmerman, a professor at Caspar College and also a Wyoming state senator.

These gatherings were always heart-warming and quite fascinating, especially for someone like myself who grew up in New York City and had little contact with small-town America, especially in its southern version. The hospitality and genuine friendliness were striking, and the hilarity was delightful. But I especially remember the attention the family gave to the explanations Sir John provided about his vision for progress in spirituality. Here were educated people who could appreciate his concern and enthusiasm for the future growth of the human spirit.

The Humility Theology Information Center

Soon after the establishment of the bylaws, Sir John began to form an advisory board for the Foundation to function within the framework of what was first called a Center for Humility Theology. The Center's research program was announced in the March 1992 issue of *Progress in Theology*:

> In recognition of the enormous impact that recent scientific research has had upon our knowledge of God's creation, the Center for Humility Theology has instituted a research program, which at present has three areas of concentration:

1. Utilization of scientific methods in understanding the work and purpose of the Creator.
2. Research on studying or stimulating progress in religion.
3. Research on the benefits of religion.

The John Templeton Foundation's resources are directed principally to operating its own program initiatives. The Center's research programs involve a broad range of projects, which include:

1. A bibliographic survey of work by scientists on spiritual subjects.
2. A program to assess the extent of teaching of university and college courses on science and religion and to stimulate courses emphasizing progress in religion.
3. A training module on religion and psychiatry that illustrates the extent to which spiritual factors impact positively on clinical therapy.
4. Templeton lectures held in the U.S. and the U.K., which explore the relationship between science and theology.[2]

Sir John received a number of letters concerning the announcement. Amid the general enthusiasm was a concern that the Foundation was seeking to establish itself as the only institution interested in humbly seeking new spiritual information. In response to this idea, Sir John decided to change the name to the Humility Theology Information Center. His thoughts were published in the September 1993 issue of the newsletter.

> In keeping with a spirit of self-examination and an eagerness to learn more about God, the Center for Humility Theology of the John Templeton Foundation has been given a new name. A few of our readers have expressed a concern that simply by designating ourselves a "Center" we are calling into question our own much-sought spirit of humility.
>
> We appreciate that criticism, and we want all people who seek progress in the knowledge of God to be assured that our quest is open-ended and that our desire is to be free of any

suggestion that we are the sole searchers for new ideas about God. The addition of the word "information" in our title is designed to emphasize the hopefully noninterpretive aspect of our Center. We want to be a useful channel for information, but at the same time we wish to avoid the restrictive language and even dogmatic assertions that often accompany theological constructions. Our hope is to be a catalyst in the search for new knowledge of God, and we see humility theology as a potentially powerful tool in such explorations.[3]

The advisory board of the Center grew quickly and included scholars in the science and religion field from many branches of science, and a few from theology. Over the years the Board has become quite diverse, with experts in comparative religion from both Harvard and Oxford, with academics of Indian extraction and the Muslim faith, and with philanthropists and journalists, publishers and political leaders as members. The list of the present advisory board members is included in Appendix B.

Honors for Sir John Templeton

Despite Sir John's diffidence and humble spirit, or maybe *because* of it, society has found ways to honor this gentle man with the uncanny eye for financial investment but an even greater vision of the spiritual future. We have mentioned his frequent appearances on *Wall Street Week,* and we can add that he has received twenty honorary degrees, as well as a very special retirement ceremony in 1985 at the end of thirty-nine years of service on the Board of Trustees of Princeton Theological Seminary. The plaque he was given simply but beautifully quoted John 1:6, "There was a man sent from God whose name was John."

Then, in 1987, he was inducted into the Imperial Society of Knights Bachelor by Queen Elizabeth II for his philanthropic work both in Britain and around the world.

John Templeton had been a British citizen since making his permanent home in the Bahamas in 1968 and so was eligible for knighthood. John Templeton has had a strong affinity for the British people, and a generous hand in their spiritual endeavors for many years, and that has not gone unnoticed. We have already mentioned the Templeton United Kingdom Trust, and the fact that the Templeton Prize was annually presented by Prince Philip, but it should also be mentioned that John has made a very significant contribution to Oxford University through Templeton College. When John had been a Rhodes scholar at Oxford, he had noted that there was no school of business at the university. So in later years, as a successful investor, he donated $5 million to the Oxford Centre for Management Studies. Then in 1984, after the Centre received an additional commitment from John of $5 million over a five year period, and an agreement from the university to allow the matriculation of twelve post-graduate students, the Centre became Templeton College. Today it is a full-fledged college of the University of Oxford.

Among other Templeton interests in Great Britain, there are two that particularly stand out. A Templeton science and religion lecture program in London, co-sponsored by the venerable Royal Society for Arts, Manufactures and Commerce (RSA), began as the result of a communication to Sir John from Christopher Lucas, director of the RSA in the fall of 1991. The RSA has had a long and distinguished history of promoting cultural interchange in Great Britain and in the various other English-speaking countries, especially the United States. With a membership of 15,000, the RSA seemed a highly desirable venue for a series of lectures on science and religion. The membership is well educated and accustomed to dealing with controversial subjects, and John could foresee the development of an excellent schedule of lectures given the outstanding speakers available from two British academic groups, the Science and Religion Forum and another religion-science organization called Christians in Science.

The facilities, too, are excellent. The RSA has its offices and conference rooms in central London, just off the Strand on John Adams Street. The building has been restored beautifully, even to the extent of providing eating facilities in a large basement area of bricked arches and exposed cobblestone floors, which may date back to its waterfront warehousing days in the sixteenth century.

Sir John asked me to organize the lectures through the American Scientific Affiliation, and I in turn asked the British-based Science and Religion Forum to carry out the planning with the RSA on behalf of the Templeton Foundation. The lecture series was presented in the fall of 1992 and the following spring, with eight lectures in all. They were well attended and the discussions spirited. Five of the lectures were published in the *RSA Journal,* which is sent to all of the 15,000 Fellows of the society.

A second Templeton program was later put together with the RSA by Templeton trustee Professor Russell Stannard of the Open University. This program opened up a valuable discussion of religious education in English schools, a controversial subject area, with professional people and policy makers throughout Great Britain.

The aftermath of these and many other Foundation activities was another honor for Sir John, the presentation of the Benjamin Franklin Medal. The occasion was a memorable one for all of us and I described it in the March 1995 newsletter.

On November 30, 1994, Sir John Templeton received the Benjamin Franklin Medal of the Royal Society of Arts, Manufactures and Commerce (RSA). The presentation was made by HRH The Prince Philip, The Duke of Edinburgh, president of the society, at a ceremony held in the reception hall of St. James Palace, London.

My wife and I were privileged to be present at the ceremony, along with some one hundred others—officers and Fellows of the RSA, Templeton Foundation staff and trustees, clergy and educators. Among the group were several lords and ladies, dukes and duchesses, and one Spanish cavalier. It was a delightful occasion, with Prince Philip adding his own special hospitality by circulating through the gathering just before the medal ceremony. Our small group introduced ourselves—though three were clergy from Windsor Castle whom he already knew well—and he asked me about my role in the Templeton Foundation. I tried to give a two-sentence description of humility theology, to which he listened patiently. Then, gesturing with his hands pointing in opposite directions, he said, "Scientists and theologians talk past each other." He obviously knows something of our problem!

The medal ceremony was short but quite moving. Sir John was being honored for his global philanthropy, especially in connection with the Templeton Prize for Progress in Religion and the Templeton U.K. Prizes, which are awarded to four British charitable and religious leaders and organizations each year. Also mentioned was Templeton College at Oxford, and the two Templeton-sponsored lecture series at the RSA.

The Benjamin Franklin Medal has an interesting history. It is an annual prize, awarded alternately to citizens of the United Kingdom and the United States who have forwarded the cause of British-American understanding. Previous recipients have included the American architects Robert Venturi and Denise Scott Brown, who designed the most recent addition to the National Gallery in London; Sir David Attenborough; and Sam Wanamaker, the American actor who has forwarded the restoration of Shakespeare's Globe Threatre on the Thames waterfront. Earlier recipients were Alistair Cooke, J. William Fullbright, Prime Minister Harold Macmillan, and famed ballerina Dame Margot Fonteyn. The Medal was originated as a result of Benjamin Franklin's contribution to the RSA's work in the 1770s as chair of the RSA's Trade and Colonies Commission, which sought to help the British people realize the importance of treating the American Colonies fairly.

Sir John's acceptance address, emphasizing the way in which Benjamin Franklin's ideals have become a strong focus of the Templeton Foundation's goals, was as follows:

"Cecil John Rhodes was the benefactor who enabled me to return to the United Kingdom, my ancestral home, from

America, the land of my birth. I was born and raised in Franklin County (Tennessee), which is one of the fifty-six United States counties and cities named in honor of Benjamin Franklin.

"It is a joy indeed to follow humbly in the footsteps of Benjamin Franklin, who tried in many ways to help the young people of these two great nations to learn more about the noble virtues. Spiritual principles and strength of character produce lives that are both useful and happy. Both Cecil John Rhodes and Benjamin Franklin would approve, I think, the programs of the Templeton Foundation and especially the new college at Rhodes' own university, Templeton College, which teaches nothing but better business management.

"It is a blessing indeed that the laws of the United Kingdom require every school to teach religious education. Really effective religious education can become a center for virtue, progress, prosperity, happiness, freedom, and spiritual growth. Such virtues will radiate automatically to all humanity.

"Courses in religious education might be more productive if they focus less on history, rituals, and differences between religions and focus more on encouraging each student to develop his own list of virtues and spiritual principles, which can make his whole life more useful and happy. Many, many such laws of life can be discovered and learned, which are self-enforcing rather than depending on authority. By collecting strong scientific evidence, many of these laws can be convincing even to skeptics. Most important of all, laws collected in this way can avoid divisiveness, sectarianism, and regionality.

"A few spiritual laws which can be supported by strong evidence are as follows.

1. Thanksgiving results in more to be thankful for.
2. The family that prays together, stays together.
3. It is more blessed to give than to receive.
4. We receive freely when we give freely.
5. It is better to love than to be loved.
6. You cannot be lonely while helping the lonely.
7. Agape given grows, agape hoarded dwindles.

8. Enthusiasm is contagious.
9. You are only as good as your word.
10. A loving person lives in a loving world.
11. Laugh and the world laughs with you; weep and you weep alone.
12. We tend to find what we look for, good or evil.
13. You can build your own heaven or hell here on earth.
14. We tend to become what we think.
15. It is better to praise than to criticize.
16. Crime does not pay.
17. If you do not know what you want to achieve with your life, you may not achieve much.

"Can every religion on earth agree on these same virtues and vices? Probably every nation can agree and also every political party. So why not help every student to learn them? Why not have examinations and grades and credit toward graduation for learning and explaining the virtues? Probably Benjamin Franklin would have been enthusiastic about this idea."

It is my sense that religious education in our public secondary schools on both sides of the Atlantic is not so much absent as it is irrelevant. Perhaps Sir John Templeton's initiative is a way to bring moral-spiritual content, the result of any good theology, back into the mainstream of Western education and Western life.[4]

Another recent celebration in which Sir John Templeton has had a major part took place at Westminster Abbey in October of 1995. The occasion was a service of dedication of the ancient cathedral after a dozen years of restoration work. Sir John had been a member of the committee chaired by Prince Philip, which raised the funds to renovate the aging structure. I was privileged to attend the ceremony and wrote this report:

Sir John Templeton was back at Westminster Abbey in October, five months after the ceremony there honoring Paul Davies as the 1995 recipient of the Templeton Prize for Progress in

Religion. This time *he* was to receive the honors, as one of the major contributors to the extensive restoration program for the Abbey which began in 1983.

This was a service of thanksgiving, with much of the rich imagery for which royal Britain is so famous. Queen Elizabeth and Prince Philip were welcomed at the Great West Door to the sound of a trumpet fanfare played by seven members of the Irish Guards. The procession which followed consisted of church officials, the Surveyor of the Fabric, the Surveyor Emeritus, the Clerk of the Works, and the group representing the many crafts involved in the restoration. After prayers and hymns and several choir offerings, Rear Admiral Kenneth Snow, secretary of the Westminster Abbey Trust, received symbols of the work—a roll of builder's drawings, a mason's mallet and chisel, a panel of painted glass, and a medallion of molded lead—and had them placed on the high altar. The procession then marched to the very ornate Lady Chapel at the rear of the church, the site of much of the restoration work. The Lady Chapel had been added to the Abbey in 1519 by Henry VII. In 1725, it became also the Chapel of the Order of the Bath, the second highest order of chivalry in England, and today holds the stalls, banners, and helmets of the Knights of the Order.

The service of dedication in the Lady Chapel focused on the new west window, which replaced a temporary clear glass window installed after the London bombings in World War II. Lord Catts, chairman of the Westminster Abbey Trust, said, "Your Majesty, on behalf of the trustees, I ask you to unveil this new west window of the Abbey's Lady Chapel, itself a gift of our fellow trustee, Sir John Templeton, to mark the completion of the restoration." The queen replied, "Mr. Dean, in thanksgiving for the restoration of our collegiate church, and in gratitude to all its benefactors and craftsmen, we commend this window to the care of the Dean and Chapter as a token of the completed work, and ask you to dedicate it."

The richly colored window contains over fifty panels of stained glass displaying the heraldic arms, ciphers, and initials of the trustees, donors, church officers, and representative craftsmen, all gathered around the Sovereign's arms in the center. Sir John Templeton's panel, with his coat of arms and his name spelled out, is at the center of the lower set of panels, just below the three-panel depiction of the Queen's coat of arms.

After the service had ended, the processors and guests moved through the adjacent cloister to a reception in the college garden. Among those received formally by the Queen were Dr. Jack Templeton, Sir John's son, and Jack's two daughters, Heather and Jennifer. It was an exciting day.

It was also a special day for the Queen, for the church, and for the nation. Westminster Abbey has been at the center of British history for over nine hundred years. It has been the setting for every coronation since 1066, and the burial place for the monarchs and saints, for great statesmen, composers, writers, poets, and scientists. Sir Isaac Newton and Charles Darwin are buried here.

But the Abbey is not just a monument to the famous, though it is visited by 3.5 million tourists each year. It has also been a place of worship and ministry ever since its beginnings as a Benedictine monastery almost a millennium ago. On the Sunday following the dedication, my wife Betty and I went back to attend church services. There in the center of the church, separated from the milling tourists, we found warmth and inspiration in the music and the Eucharist. Somehow, the great events of the past few days and the past few centuries did not detract. We were all on the same humble pilgrimage to meet our God.

As we worshipped there, it seemed to us that progress in our theology would somehow always need to preserve this continuity with the past, with those whose hands are raised in worship, and with those whose hands fashion stone and glass.[5]

In 1992 Sir John was honored with a festschrift, a collection of articles by some of his most respected friends and colleagues, with a foreword written by His Royal Highness, the Duke of Edinburgh. Prince Philip wrote:

29 November 1992

Dear Sir John,

The world is full of experts and specialists, but it is given to few to be pluralists; those exceptional people who not only comprehend the great issues, but whose questing minds can go straight to the heart of the matter. Your highly successful business career and the wide scope of your interests bear witness to both the clarity and originality of your thoughts. You have backed this up with a truly magnificent generosity to the many causes close to your heart.

It is not the passionate revolutionaries who improve the world; the only genuine progress is made by those who have a clearer vision and a greater ability to see through the tangled web of humbug and convention. Your great contribution to human civilisation has been to encourage people to concentrate on the things that really matter and to appraise both conventional as well as unconventional ideas for their true worth.

No one person can change the world by themselves, but each one of us can strive to leave the world a slightly better place. Many do strive, but in your long life you have succeeded in making this world a better place both for present and future generations.

Yours sincerely,
Philip
Buckingham Palace

These were warm words for John Templeton, who has indeed been a great encourager, believing that we all have God-given abilities to develop and use, and, as Prince Philip implies, the aggregate of our efforts will leave the world a better place.

One of John's favorite passages of Scripture is from Luke's gospel, from Jesus' Sermon on the Mount.

But alas for you who are rich: you are having your consolation now.

Alas for you who have your fill now: you shall go hungry.

Alas for you who laugh now: you shall mourn and weep.

Alas for you when the world speaks well of you! This was the way their ancestors treated the false prophets.

But I say this to you who are listening: Love your enemies, do good to those who hate you, bless those who curse you, pray for those who treat you badly. To the man who slaps you on one cheek, present the other cheek too; to the man who takes your cloak from you, do not refuse your tunic. Give to everyone who asks you, and do not ask for your property back from the man who robs you. Treat others as you would like them to treat you. If you love those who love you, what thanks can you expect? Even sinners lend to sinners to get back the same amount. Instead, love your enemies and do good, and lend without any hope of return. You will have a great reward, and you will be sons of the Most High, for he himself is kind to the ungrateful and the wicked. (Luke 6:24–35)

Based upon this passage, what Sir John Templeton would perhaps add to Prince Philip's words is the special place of both humility and love in our dealings with each other. It is a passage that John Marks Templeton has made foundational in his own life.

CHAPTER 13

The Future of The Vision

The Staff of the John Templeton Foundation

 In 1988, Frances Schapperle, the lone staff member of the John Templeton Foundation, began her work in an office in the garden house of Dr. Jack Templeton's home in Bryn Mawr, Pennsylvania. Frances arrived with excellent credentials from the Robert Wood Johnson Foundation, but the job before her was a daunting one. Perhaps the most demanding part of the job was the large amount of travel as she divided her time between Sir John's home in Lyford Cay, Nassau and the Bryn Mawr office. But, the most challenging aspect was the responsibility for the large number of projects with which Sir John was engaged and the variety of his interests as a world philanthropist. His projects in those early years already spanned the globe—most notably in the variety of winners of the Templeton Prize for Progress in Religion but also in prizes and donations to hospitals and churches on five continents.

By 1992, the number of major projects supported by the Foundation grew to twenty and by 1997 had reached sixty-five. Frances found needed support in a very capable colleague, Judith Marchand, a former University of Pennsylvania Foundation staff member who joined the Templeton Foundation in 1991. Since then the office has moved to the

Radnor Corporate Center, a large complex in another part of suburban Philadelphia, and the number of staff has grown to twenty.

Sir John hopes this new group of experts will enhance the future of his vision of achieving new spiritual information through scientific research. Foremost in this thinking is the promise of the new executive director and senior vice president, Dr. Charles Harper, who came to the Foundation in September of 1996. He was recruited from a large number of candidates to replace Frances Schapperle, who moved to California because of family relocation, but who remains a vice president and also serves as the western representative for the Foundation. Charles Harper's employment came as a result of Sir John's unusual recruitment strategy. A former Rhodes scholar himself, Sir John contacted all the younger Rhodes scholars to inquire of their interest in the executive director position. Dr. Harper's wife, a former Rhodes scholar, received one of the letters; thus began the contact that would bring Dr. Harper on board.

Charles Harper was eminently suited for the job. He was trained in both science and theology, earning a bachelor's degree in civil and geological engineering at Princeton, a doctorate of philosophy in cosmology and planetary science at Balliol College, and a diploma of theology from Balliol College and Wycliffe Hall at Oxford. Prior to coming to the Foundation, he was a research scientist at Harvard University and a research fellow with the National Aeronautics and Space Administration in Houston.

Dr. Harper has published more than fifty papers and abstracts in scientific journals and he brings to the Foundation an unusual level of tireless energy, which is not unlike Sir John's. I personally have found him quite impressive, with broad knowledge in philosophy and the humanities, yet also warm and considerate and deeply committed to Sir John's vision.

The other new staff member, Rev. Dr. Bryant Kirkland, vice president, is the former much-beloved minister of the

Fifth Avenue Presbyterian Church in New York City. He had been a trustee of the Foundation for several years, but stepped down to take the staff position last year. He too brings great sagacity, warmth, and commitment to the job. Dr. Kirkland was educated at Wheaton College and Princeton Seminary and has since been president of the American Bible Society and president of the Board of Trustees of Princeton Theological Seminary. He also brings great experience to the Foundation as vast sources are sought to achieve Sir John's goal of the expenditure of ten million dollars per day for progress in spiritual information through scientific research.

The remainder of the Radnor senior staff includes the veteran Judy Marchand, now senior program officer; her assistant Laura Molina; Pam Lairdieson as controller; Karyl Wittlinger as office manager and conference coordinator; Dr. Arthur Schwartz as the director of the "Laws of Life" Essay Contests and Character-building Programs for the past two years; and Joanna Hill, as director of publications, whose role we will discuss later in this chapter.

In Lyford Cay in Nassau, Sir John has two very able assistants: Mena Griffiths, vice president of Sir John's First Trust Bank, who has been with John for twenty-five years; and Irish-born Mary Walker, who has ably assisted Sir John for nineteen years. Also in the Lyford Cay office is Rev. Wilbert Forker, formerly an officer of the World Council of Churches, who has been the director of the Templeton Prize for Progress in Religion Program with the wise assistance of Mena Griffiths.

In Tennessee, the official home of the Templeton Foundation, are two principal officers, Ann Templeton Cameron, secretary, and Harvey Templeton III, treasurer. They are the children of Harvey and Jewel Templeton of Winchester, Tennessee.

Those of us who have been fortunate to be trustees of the John Templeton Foundation have had the privilege of meeting many of these staff people, especially at the annual trustees' meetings in Monteagle, Tennessee each summer.

The Advisory Board of the Humility Theology Information Center

During the first year of the Foundation's existence Sir John began to develop a Board of Advisors to aid in the formulation of programs and, in some cases, to participate in programs themselves. Because of Sir John's concern for good science as the backbone of a spiritual research program, many of the Advisors chosen were working scientists with a commitment to integrate their science into the spiritual dimension of their lives. Many advisors are or were connected with organizations that have this integration as a major goal, including the American Scientific Affiliation, the Center for Theology and the Natural Sciences, the Chicago Center for Religion and Science, the Christian Medical and Dental Society, the British organization called Christians in Science, the European Society for the Study of Science and Theology, the Institute for Religion in an Age of Science, and another British organization, the Science and Religion Forum.

All of the major scientific disciplines have been represented on the Advisory Board. Some of the most notable were Owen Gingerich, a Harvard astronomer, historian of science, and Smithsonian Fellow; Princeton physicist Freeman Dyson of the Institute for Advanced Study; Nobel laureate Sir John Eccles, a neurophysiologist then at the Max Planck Institute, Heidelberg; and Nobel laureate Charles Townes, a physicist at the University of California, Berkeley. Also well-known are Herbert Benson, a Harvard Medical School professor and president of the Mind-Body Institute; and V. Elving Anderson, professor of genetics at the University of Minnesota and former president of the Society of Sigma Xi, the national research honorary.

In addition, the Board includes several individuals holding degrees in both science and theology, including physicist Robert Russell of the Center for Theology and the Natural Sciences who is also an ordained minister in the Church of Christ; and Ian Barbour, Professor of Physics and Professor of Religion at Carleton College. Likewise, Karl Schmitz-Moormann, first president of the European Society for the Study of Science and Theology, was a theologian who had spent a lifetime studying the paleontological and theological work of Pierre Teilhard de Chardin. In addition, two British scientists, biochemist Arthur Peacocke and physicist John Polkinghorne, are advisors. Peacocke had been a working scientist at Birmingham and Oxford in the field of the physical chemistry of biological macromolecules for twenty years and was ordained as a priest in the Church of England in 1971. Polkinghorne was chair of mathematical physics at Cambridge and had a career in particle physics for twenty-five years before resigning to train for the Anglican ministry in 1979. He is a Fellow of the Royal Society and was recently knighted by Her Majesty Queen Elizabeth.

The advisory board has met each spring and fall in two sets of meetings—one in the United States for North American Advisors and the other in London for the Advisors from the United Kingdom, the Continent, and Australia. Since 1996, under the guidance of Foundation Executive Director Charles Harper, the Board has held two-day meetings prior to the regular Board meeting to review scientific progress and research directions in various areas of science especially relevant to theology. In addition, individual advisors consult with the Foundation on the various programs. A list of the current members of the advisory board is included in Appendix B.

Main Objectives of the John Templeton Foundation

Sir John Templeton set out the current objectives of the Foundation in December of 1996. These generally took the form of broad statements of purpose, and it will be my goal in this final chapter to describe the way in which these objectives are being interpreted and are beginning to be implemented by the Foundation staff. As usual, Sir John's vision is vast and far-reaching in scope, and the present chapter can only hope to anticipate a few of the developments that will result from his plans.

1. The first objective is to encourage progress in obtaining new spiritual information that rivals the progress that has been made in obtaining medical and other scientific information.

When the National Institutes of Health began its major extramural program in support of medical and biological research, no one could have dreamed of the progress that would result in information about the human body and about the diagnosis and treatment of disease in only forty years. Indeed, whole new areas of interdisciplinary research have appeared, including

- Human genetic research with the goal of sequencing the entire human genome and the beginning of treatment of a broad range of human genetic diseases;
- Brain research including the goal of developing means for treatment of degenerative brain disease by brain tissue transplantation and regeneration;
- Immunological studies of tissue transplantation leading to effective means of heart and liver transplantation; and
- Neuroendocrinology research elucidating the interaction of the hormonal and nervous systems in promoting recovery from and resistance to disease.

In the case of brain research, the results of recent brain developmental studies indicate that the brain, heretofore thought to be static and unchanging, is actually an active, dynamic, ever changing structure, which even in adulthood responds to new experiences and new learning patterns. The current viewpoint is that the brain is remarkably plastic in character, responsive to stimuli by generating new neuronal networks, and even capable of regenerating old networks such as those lost in Parkinson's disease.

Sir John argues that significant research support for the acquisition of new spiritual information could be even more beneficial. Here are just a few examples of the thousands of questions that might be addressed.

- *Human evolution.* Studies have shown that late Neanderthals and early Homo sapiens had definite ideas of a hereafter, which were reflected in their burial practices and cave drawings. Further research might establish the fundamental nature of this spiritual understanding.
- *Genetic basis for well-being.* Dr. Herbert Benson has analyzed the nature of some spiritual factors in healing and has proposed that we are hardwired for wellness. Research could be carried out to study wellness as a genetic trait or group of traits.
- *Brain capacity.* Neural science indicates we utilize less than 10 percent of our brain capacity. Research of the biochemical basis of genius and creativity, especially with the great mystics and the Nobel laureates, might be revealing and suggest ways to unlock the potential of the brain.
- *Neuroendocrine relationships.* Research into spiritual activities (e.g., prayer, meditation, and especially thanksgiving) to ascertain various hormone release actions—endorphins and other "pleasure" agents—might establish a basis for spiritual experience as an alternative to various psychoactive drugs (e.g., cocaine and heroin) currently ravaging society.
- *Violence as a social problem.* Research into genetic and neurological bases for anti-social behavior is an area of political sensitivity, but scientifically rigorous research might arrive at much-needed understanding and possible therapies.

2. The Foundation's second objective is to encourage the idea that no human has yet known one percent of God, the basic Reality, but that we can learn more about God in many ways through rigorous scientific research.

This second objective is closely aligned to the first, but the emphasis now shifts to the recognition that we are pitifully ignorant of the fundamental Reality that is God, and that doors are now open to explore many new avenues in our pursuit of spiritual information. Some of our approaches may involve careful statistical studies as in the attempt to correlate spirituality and health. Other approaches may involve psychological studies, as in some research on the "Laws of Life."

The initial plan is to concentrate on a few representative areas, delineating the kinds of approaches and demonstrating the multitude of questions that can be asked within any one approach. As will be discussed in more detail later, Sir John sees the mobilization of the university scientific community for this effort as possibly crucial. Leading scientists may be asked to propose research methodologies and to provide expert review of proposals.

3. The third objective is to encourage the expenditure of at least one-tenth as much on obtaining spiritual information as is spent on all scientific research. This is an ambitious goal. The world spends approximately one billion dollars a day now on scientific research. To even begin to achieve support at one-tenth this level will require the recruitment of enormous funding from many sources. The pursuit of spiritual information needs to capture the imagination of opinion makers and scientific planners throughout the world.

Partners in the Templeton Foundation-sponsored programs may be found among the nation's traditional science supporters if the work planned is rigorous and well peer-reviewed. The National Institutes of Health, especially through the Human Genome initiative, the National Institute for Mental Health, and the National Institute on Aging could become strong allies in this research area. The new office of Alternative Medicine at NIH could find studies of spirituality and health an attractive fruitful focus for support.

4. Another objective for the Foundation is to study the possibility that the visible and tangible are only tiny manifestations of the vast timeless and limitless Reality. Here, current research in physics and cosmology, as described by scientists such as Paul Davies and Robert Russell, reveals that Reality is

vastly greater and more mysterious than we had thought. In a recent book titled *How Large is God?*, edited by Sir John, several contributors lend support to the vastness and infinitude of Reality. My own chapter, entitled "How Large is God? How Deep is Reality?" testifies to the fleeting nature of scientific reality. In the conclusion to that chapter I wrote:

> We have seen that science has gone through a healthy re-evaluation of its understanding of the nature of truth over the past two decades. No longer would most scientists claim that their theories represent anything more than approximations of the structures of reality. We have looked also at some of the current research in physics and chemistry and found that our goal of simplification and unification has been thwarted by drastic limitations in our capacity to provide experiential verification and by undreamt of levels of complexity in the systems under study.
>
> The present situation in the sciences seems to shout for caution in our statements of what is, and how it came to be. What seems abundantly clear is that reality is much deeper and more profound than we had thought. Clerk Maxwell appears to have been "on the mark" when he suggested that appropriateness and tenability of scientific theories might best be evaluated by whether they measured up as far as possible to the "riches of creation." If we are attempting to think the Creator's thoughts, our thoughts must surely be only the simplest inklings of what really lies behind this vast universe and its awesome Creator.[1]

5. Sir John's next objective is to study the probability that nothing exists separate from God and that we may be tiny temporary manifestations of God just as a wave of the ocean is not separate from the ocean but is only a tiny temporary manifestation of that ocean.

This concept was elaborated as the first point in the Foundation bylaws description of Humility Theology. Sir John first introduced the idea of a progression from biological life to the sphere of the human intellect and then to the sphere of the spirit.

Perhaps this heralds a new quality, the sphere of the spirit. God may be creating not only the infinitely large but also the infinitely small; not only the outward but also the inward; not only the tangible but also the intangible. Thoughts, mind, soul, wisdom, love, originality, inspiration, and enthusiasm may be little manifestations of a Creator who is omniscient, omnipotent, eternal, and infinite. The things that we see, hear, and touch may be only appearances. They may be only manifestations of underlying forces, including spiritual forces which may persist throughout all the transience of physical existence. Perhaps the spiritual world, and the benevolent Creator whom it reflects, may be the only reality.

Presumably the sphere of the spirit may enclose not only this planet but the entire universe, and so God is all of Nature, is inseparable from it, and yet exceeds it. Perhaps it is mankind's own ego that leads us to think that we are at the center of a vast universe of being which subsists in an eternal and infinite reality which some call God. Maybe all of nature is only a transient wave on the ocean of all that God eternally is. Maybe time, space, and energy provide no limit to the Being which is God. Likewise the fundamental parameters of the universe—the speed of light, the force of gravitation, the weak and strong nuclear forces, and electromagnetism—would seem to pose no limits to the Being which is God.

Experiments such as the famous double-slit experiment, which we described in *The God Who Would Be Known*,[2] suggest that there is indeed a wholeness about the universe, an interconnectedness, a higher kind of order.

Can the Foundation find ways to further encourage scientific studies of wholeness, perhaps supporting further studies of cooperativity in reaction systems and new approaches to interference phenomena?

6. The next goal is to study evidence that God is creative and purposeful and that our role may be to be an agent of progress for God's purposes.

Sir John has already edited a book titled *Evidence of Purpose*, which includes essays from outstanding contributors in various scientific fields. In his introduction, he wrote:

There is here no knockdown argument for design and purpose, but certainly there are strong hints of ultimate realities beyond the cosmos, just as Owen Gingerich says in his chapter. One of the strongest hints, in our opinion, relates to the new understanding of the creativity of the cosmos, its capacity for so-called self-organization. For, following the Big Bang, a most astounding story of creativity unfolds throughout time, from the void of space to galaxies, planets, crystals, life, and people. Science has heretofore been ruled by the Newtonian and thermodynamic paradigms, viewing the universe as either an unchanging and static machine, or as a process moving inexorably toward degeneration and decay. But current science leads us to look for a new paradigm, a universe fraught with creativity in the direction of cooperative and organizational processes. The gradual growth of complexity has been noted throughout the history of science, but it was given powerful support through the theory of biological evolution proposed by Charles Darwin and Alfred Russel Wallace. Subsequent developments in cosmological science have demonstrated that the increased complexity and diversity inherent in biological evolution have also been characteristic of the entire universe from its origin. Indeed, there appears to be a continuity of organization into novel and increasingly complex structures and relationships throughout the spectrum of transitions from stardust to thinking man. How did these changes come about? What processes are involved?[3]

The new studies of nonlinear thermodynamics provide insights into such creativity, and further studies of evolutionary processes may add more data about this remarkably creative phenomenon. The Foundation hopes to be in the forefront of these new scientific investigations.

7. The Foundation's next goal is to encourage rigorous study by scientific methods of some of the "Laws of Life" and to apply those proving valid to character-building courses in universities and colleges. In this way, education in moral development might be allowed to go forward in secular institutions that are prohibited from using the teachings of ancient scripture.

The first request for proposals for research on the "Laws of Life" focused on the phenomenon of forgiveness. The June 9, 1997 draft of the announcement read:

> The John Templeton Foundation seeks to stimulate progress in science, particularly by encouraging the appreciation of an open, humble, and empirical approach to developing new aspects of spiritual and moral understanding. Through this request for proposal (RFP) we seek to sponsor innovative, methodologically rigorous scientific research in the area of forgiveness; enhance the scientific understanding of moral and spiritual principles; and stimulate the growth of new understanding in this area of research. The Foundation is open to considerations of a wide range of approaches and methodologies relevant to the study of forgiveness in many contexts. Extensive information on the Founder's vision and publications, and on the mission and activities of the John Templeton Foundation may be found on the John Templeton Foundation's webpage (www.templeton.org).
>
> Scope of the Proposed Research: Examples of areas of interest include: studies of individual health and happiness; studies relating to the health and stability of marriages, families, neighborhoods and communities; studies relating to the development of character in children and youth; studies relating to racial and ethnic conflict, as well as studies relating to the role of forgiveness in business, legal, political, and historical contexts. Research projects should involve empirical examinations rather than philosophical or ethical or theological investigations, except in relation to the development of testable hypotheses or models involving human subjects. (In exemplary cases, proposals for innovative primate studies will be considered.) Applications from a broad range of disciplines are sought, and interdisciplinary collaboration is strongly encouraged.
>
> Research focusing on the development of habits of forgiveness as a *spiritual discipline* and the appreciation of forgiveness as a *spiritual principle* are especially encouraged. Researchers are also encouraged to investigate biological aspects of forgiveness as well as proposing projects posing criti-

cal challenges to forgiveness as applied in particular circumstances.

Objectivity and analytical rigor is stressed. Investigators involved in advocacy must be particularly exacting in their methodological design in order to avoid biasing their research findings.

When this research initiative was developing, the Templeton Foundation Press published Sir John's latest book on the laws of life, *Worldwide Laws of Life: 200 Eternal Spiritual Principles.* In addition, the *New York Times* Syndicate bought the right to publish a weekly column with Sir John's byline, to continue each week for a year, with one law of life featured each week.

Sir John also looks to the possible development of academic courses utilizing the *Worldwide Laws of Life,* and welcomes research proposals from established scientists for evidence to verify or falsify any of these laws.

Other ongoing programs of the Foundation include the Templeton Honor Roll for Character-Building Colleges and the "Laws of Life" Essay Contests. The latter, focusing on teenagers, now reaches 34,000 school-age youngsters in the United Kingdom, the Bahamas, and thirty-five American school districts. Another twenty school districts plan to begin a contest soon.

Sir John is pleased with the reception given the "Laws of Life" approach to character building. He hopes that *Worldwide Laws of Life* will be extensively translated for use in Europe and Asia. Already an earlier version of the book is being published in Russian.

8. Another objective is to encourage rigorous research by scientists about spiritual benefits to health and to extend these results to medical school educators.

Two major programs are already in progress, one carried on by the National Institute for Healthcare Research (NIHR) and the other by the Mind-Body Medical Institute of Harvard Medical School. The NIHR is developing a network of highly competent research fellows whose research programs will be enhanced through Foundation funds and other sources. The Mind-Body Medical Institute is also developing a major network of researchers and is helping graduate programs in a number of major medical institutions.

Both NIHR and the Mind-Body Medical Institute have convened highly successful conferences of researchers and health-care providers to emphasize the opportunities for a major impact on disease through spiritual therapies. These conferences are developing into regular yearly series.

Medical school education will be helped further by expanding the program of prizes for courses in medicine and religion currently being administered through NIHR.

9. Another Templeton objective is to encourage university and college courses integrating science and religion. The current Science Religion Course program has just awarded 97 more prizes, making a total of 294 courses in universities, colleges, and seminaries worldwide that have received prizes of $10,000 each. Forty-one awards went to state and private universities, a considerable increase from previous years, indicating that the science-religion course program is gaining support in the secular academic community.

Future goals are to strengthen the newly constituted regional programs in each of the six regions where course training workshops are held. Conferences explaining the program in various major academic centers will be extended to many more localities in the coming years. Future workshop sites in South Africa, Australia, India, and Poland are planned. A German conference at Heidelberg has been funded to bring German theologians and scientists together to begin to plan courses in science and religion in German universities.

Sir John projects that the Science Religion Course program may have well over one thousand courses in place by the year 2000. Several forms of developmental funding are planned for past winners to provide for their continued improvement as scholars.

10. The Foundation also seeks to enhance education in virtue, ethics, and good character development.

The "Laws of Life" Essay contests mentioned previously represent a significant beginning in education for character development. Likewise, the Templeton Honor Role for Character-Building Colleges, which began in 1989 and has to date highlighted more than 350 colleges and universities with significant character-building programs, has played an important part.

The Foundation is considering developing a large-scale program of prizes for academic courses emphasizing character building, moral development, and personal ethics.

11. Sir John also plans to provide more yearly honors and prizes at the level of the Pulitzer Prize for the production of positive and inspirational programs and articles in the media. Some say the media—especially television—has become increasingly negative, anti-religious, and focused on violence. Significant prizes for uplifting and inspirational programs will be very important.

Past awards have been directed to religious editors and to Christian television producers. Another goal is to extend such prizes to religious radio broadcasters and movie critics. In the long run, helping journalism schools in leading universities to give faculty awards for teaching positive journalism may have a beneficial impact.

12. Another objective is to encourage university research worldwide for new spiritual information and to enhance its publication in books and in peer-reviewed journals.

The Exemplary Papers Program, as the Call for Papers on Humility Theology Program is now called, will be enlarged and extended, and many of its prize-winning papers published in the *Reader's Supplement* of the *Progress in Theology* newsletter.

As mentioned earlier, the Foundation has a request-for-proposal program for research on forgiveness. Other "Laws of Life" principles will shortly be added as subjects for research, including studies of thanksgiving and of agape love. As with the program for research on forgiveness, these proposals must be of high quality, utilizing rigorous scientific methodologies and must be designed for publication in quality scientific journals.

Another program, the Science and Spiritual Quest Program, helps to bring outstanding scientists from a variety of religious backgrounds together for discussion of mutual interests and concerns. The program's director, Mark Richardson, describes its goals as follows:

> Is there life on Mars, and if so, does it indicate life's inevitability in a universe such as this? Do baboons and other primates have compassion and moral codes, and if so, in what way is this informative regarding human beings and their similarities with other mammals, and/or their uniqueness?
>
> These are just two questions among many others to surface in recent months in scientific news stories across the country. They show the increasing frequency of events and discoveries, which lead scientific inquiry to consider questions regarding ultimate meaning and value—questions which science alone cannot answer.
>
> The Science and Spiritual Quest Program, directed by the Center for Theology and the Natural Sciences (CTNS), plans to explore these boundaries with teams of scientists in physics, cosmology, biology, and computer-information technologies. They will reflect on the connections between their work and long-standing religious and spiritual visions of life. The first workshop will be in the spring of 1997, followed by a second workshop in the winter. These will build toward a major public conference, to be held in the spring of 1998.[4]

At this point the four groups have met and the plan is moving forward.

In addition, a program to help university researchers in the arena of science and religion has just been proposed by the Foundation. It is called the Humble Approach Initiative, and is also designed to bring top scientists together in small intimate conferences to consider some of the wide-open possibilities that the joining of scientific and theological ideas makes possible. It is planned to seek partial funding from outside agencies for organization of these consultations, which may occur at the rate of ten per year over a five-year period. The ideas that may be addressed by these working groups are many and varied:

- Complexity and Purpose in the Universe
- "Laws of Life": The Mathematical Biology of Moral Behavior
- *Homo Religiosus:* The Contribution of Neuroscience, Genetics, Anthropology, and Evolutionary Biology toward Understanding the Role and Significance of Human Spirituality
- The Evolution of the Brain and the Origins of Religion: An Inquiry into the Roots of Human Nature
- The Uses and Abuses of Scientific Reductionism: A Critical Issue for Science and Religion
- Truth and Beauty in the Universe: Is There a Purpose for Which it Exists?
- First International Congress on Forgiveness Research
- Neuroimmunology and the Faith Factor in Human Health
- Love and the Ultimate Nature of Reality
- Thinking about the Big Picture: The Hubble Deep Field and Our Evolving View of the Universe
- Being Thankful: Developing a Research Strategy for Understanding the Power of Gratitude
- Game Theory and Theological Metaphysics
- *The Book of Nature:* Old Theologies and New Perspectives for Enriching the Encounter of Evangelicalism with Science

13. Another of Sir John's plans is to provide prizes for journalists and other media people for articles and programs illustrating that prosperity, progress, and peace result in those

nations which encourage freedom in enterprise, competition, information, communication, travel, religion, and research.

The Foundation has addressed this goal with a proposal for a new academic course program, to be called the Visions of Freedom Project, which is based on the following five theses:

- Freedom is a complex, multi-faceted topic. The goal of guiding students in the development of a nuanced understanding of freedom and its attendant responsibilities is worthy and commendable. It almost unavoidably calls for interdisciplinary approaches in course teaching.
- The topic of freedom leads readily to some form of coalescence of several domains of scholarship, including political history; the history of ideas/intellectual history; economic history and the history of economic thought; legal/constitutional history; educational history; moral philosophy; political philosophy; religion, theology and religious freedom; and the role of freedom in art and literature.
- Debate and dialogue are especially appropriate modes of teaching on the topic of freedom. A healthy, open, pedagogically creative environment is most likely to be achieved when the teaching team encompasses a wide diversity of opinion, especially on the political spectrum, and is able to demonstrate a high standard of orderly collegial debate.
- Quality in teaching a course on freedom and responsibility is enhanced when considerations of philosophical views are illuminated by careful surveys of empirical evidence, whenever relevant.
- The development of an international teaching project will provide a stimulus for curricular development and, most importantly, for the nurturing of a large and diverse community of scholars with broad interdisciplinary expertise suitable for teaching the topic of freedom

eventually without the need for a special program of support.

Some major features of the proposed program are:

- To launch courses at some ten distinguished institutions to provide a range of models of excellence;
- To establish a worldwide prize competition overseen by distinguished scholars;
- To establish common "core texts" to allow for a world-wide student examination prize competition; and
- To organize a parallel workshop program to be called the Templeton Institute for the Advanced Study of Freedom to support high quality faculty development.

14. Another Templeton objective is to honor and reward universities worldwide that take the lead in education for character development.

The Foundation is continuing and enlarging the scope of its program titled the Templeton Honor Roll for Education in a Free Society, which serves to highlight individuals and institutions that most exemplify the ideals of education in freedom. The recent awards luncheon in Washington, D.C., attended by Milton Friedman, Gertrude Himmelfarb, and William Bennett as honored guests, drew a large audience of governmental and media people.

15. John Templeton also hopes to encourage a spirit of humility within all the great religions. Three programs of the Foundation address this objective directly. The recent winner of the Templeton Prize for Progress in Religion, Pandurang Athavale, is a good example of a humble man of the Hindu faith who emphasizes that God is in every human being regardless of caste or economic status. His ministry has been the means to transform a significant part of Indian society. His testimony and the Foundation's recognition through the Templeton Prize is one more example of how all religions should "sit down together."

In addition, the Foundation's Science and Spiritual Quest Program, described under the twelfth objective, seeks to bring scientists of different religious persuasions together for mutual sharing and understanding.

Finally, the Foundation's Science & Religion Course Program encourages faculty at universities and colleges who emphasize Judaism, Islam, Buddhism, and other Eastern religions to participate in the program.

16. Sir John also hopes to publicize the multiplying blessings of the benefits of the challenges we face through the creation of a new publishing program. The inauguration of the Foundation's own publishing organization, Templeton Foundation Press, was related in the newsletter, *Progress in Theology*:

> On December 10, 1996, Sir John Templeton, John M. Templeton, Jr., M.D., and the trustees of the John Templeton Foundation announced the inauguration of the Templeton Foundation Press, which will publish books in the areas of religion and science, moral education, and the scientific verification of basic spiritual principles. Joanna Hill, formerly marketing manager at the Swedenborg Foundation, has been named director of publications. Books will be distributed in the U.S. by the Continuum Publishing Group, and outside the U.S. by SPCK.
>
> "Templeton Foundation Press is dedicated to the same principles as the Templeton Foundation and the Templeton Prize for Progress in Religion," said Sir John Templeton on the launch of the publishing venture held in New York City. "This new branch of the Foundation presents us with another venue for supporting ongoing exploration of the vital connections between religious principles and scientific research. The books that will be published under the imprint will promote a deeper understanding of the influence of spirituality, beliefs, and values on human health, happiness, and prosperity."
>
> The first book to be published as a Templeton Foundation Press title will be *Worldwide Laws of Life* by John Marks Templeton (June 1997).[5]

About Joanna Hill a press release announced:

The John Templeton Foundation has named Joanna Hill director of publications, a new position for the Foundation. Prior to her appointment, Hill worked at the North Carolina, Texas, and Louisiana State University Presses, was production manager at the Jewish Publication Society, and worked as marketing manager at the Swedenborg Foundation. "Sir John's vision offers exciting possibilities for publishing" says Hill. "I see us doing a combination of trade and scholarly books that focus on spirituality, science, and religion; health and healing; and character building. The scientific/religious interests of the John Templeton Foundation will be reflected in the list; in fact, some of the manuscripts will come as a result of grants and funding provided to scholars by the Foundation."

The Foundation has already co-published or sponsored more than two dozen books on science and religion, including the recent *Discovering the Laws of Life, The Humble Approach, Is God the Only Reality?*, and *The God Who Would Be Known,* all by Sir John Templeton. Other titles include *Who's Who in Theology and Science, 1996 Edition* and *Looking Forward: The Next Forty Years,* edited by Templeton.

The Foundation's books are distributed by the Continuum Publishing Group. Kenneth Giniger, publishing consultant to the Foundation, will coordinate his activities with Hill and the Foundation to develop its list of trade and scholarly books.[6]

Among the books Sir John has written are three books directly relevant to this objective. One is *Is Progress Speeding Up?: Our Multiplying Multitudes of Blessings,* and a second is *Golden Nuggets from Sir John Templeton.* The third book is *Riches for the Mind and Spirit: John Marks Templeton's Treasury of Words to Help, Inspire and Live By.*

Another publication effort of the Foundation is *Progress in Theology,* an eight-page newsletter of the Humility Theology Information Center of the John Templeton Foundation. It has been published quarterly for the past three years but was recently expanded to six news issues and two readers' supplements in order to cover the expanding programs of the Foundation.

Also planned is the next edition (third edition) of *Who's Who in Theology and Science,* an international compilation of scholars working in the interdisciplinary field of science and religion.

17. Another objective outlined in Sir John's December 1996 memo is to enhance the impact and public awareness of the Templeton Prize for Progress in Religion. The prize has been a centerpiece of Sir John's emphasis on progress in new spiritual information, and it may well help increasing numbers of people while the Foundation's many programs attract more and more media attention. Some thought is currently being given to revising the guidelines used by the panel of judges who select the prize winners. Many of us felt that the science-religion interaction should be further emphasized, and that more of the winners could be scientists.

Conclusion

John Templeton's vision of the future is of a world alive to the realization that we are all spiritual beings; that we have been fashioned out of what appears material but is, in reality, more accurately described by science as a unique conjunction of wave patterns, material substance in appearance but spiritual beings in reality. If this is our true nature, he says, then perhaps the most important thing we could ever know is the extent of and the meaning of our spiritual selves and our relationship to the Creator God of the Universe. Given the enormous success of the scientific approach thus far in our probing of this universe, Sir John's call to focus one-tenth of our research expenditures on the spiritual dimension would seem to be the best investment recommendation ever made.

This vision of his has not come about by happenstance. John Templeton's life has been marked by a special combination of spiritual influences: prayer, a God-generated discipline, love of all people, and a humble and thankful spirit. John Templeton has derived great strength from a regular prayer life, not only evidenced at all his investment company meetings, but in his private life as well. For the past ten years he has committed his life, family, and enterprises to God each morning. Here are parts of his daily prayers, prayed each morning for the past twelve years:

Almighty God, our loving heavenly Father, through faith and the Holy Ghost I am totally one unity with Thee. I am completely whole in mind and body.

Thou art all of me and I am a little part of Thee. Every little cell, every little vibration which is me is only an outward expression of Thy divine will in perfect health and harmony.

Thou art always guiding me, inspiring me to make the right decisions in family matters, in business matters, in health matters, and especially in spiritual matters.

And dear God, I am deeply, deeply grateful for Thy millions of blessings and millions of miracles with which you surround each of us.

Today and every day, I am especially grateful for the miracle of prayers answered and for the joy of being a humble servant of Thine on earth.

Help me to see more clearly how to use these marvelously increasing assets and talents to accomplish the very most for Thy purposes on earth.

Dear God, help me to open my mind and heart more fully to receive Thy unlimited love and wisdom, and to radiate these to Thy other children on earth especially today and every day this year.

And thank Thee dear God for blessing and protecting all my travels and public appearances so that all will be safe, on time, and useful.

Dear God, thank Thee for blessing and inspiring each person concerned with the Templeton programs to help religion and freedom.

Thank Thee for my redemption and salvation and for Thy gift of the Holy Ghost by grace, which fills me to overflowing and increasingly dominates my every thought and word and deed.

To Thee we pray in the name of Thy beloved son whom I adore and seek to imitate, my savior and my God, Christ Jesus. Amen.

John Templeton's disciplined life has long been based on an assurance that God rewards the worker whose motivation is to serve the high calling of spiritual blessing for all of mankind. Whether in the role of investment counselor or seminary trustee or Foundation executive, John has displayed a tireless commitment to this goal. Anyone who has worked with him marvels at his incredibly tight schedule and his refusal to waste a precious moment. He always carries something in his pocket to read or review in case there is a free minute. Yet he will always make time if you need his advice or counsel.

Perhaps John's most salient desire—to love all people—produces the most powerful influence of his life. For out of this deeply spiritual motivation comes a humble attitude toward his fellow man and a reasonable appraisal of his own remarkable talents. And this attitude, as we have emphasized in this book, leads to that most remarkable goal, humility theology. As John's vision has revealed it, humility toward God is the key to our spiritual blessing. As we recognize how little we know of the Creator of this enormous and intricate universe, the opportunity presents itself to explore our knowledge of God and our spiritual future in a new and powerful way. This is what John Templeton cherishes for our future.

Appendixes

Awards and Accomplishments of John Marks Templeton

1967–1973	President of the Board of Trustees of Princeton Theological Seminary
1973	Founded the Templeton Prizes for Progress in Religion
1979	Recipient of the Churchman of the Year Award from the Religious Heritage of America
1981	International Churchman of the Year Award
1981	Ecumenical Patriarch's Honorary Order of Mount Athos
1984	Free Enterprise Award, Palm Beach Atlantic College
1984	Founded Templeton UK Project Trust
1987	Knight Order of the British Empire
1987	Centennial Medal of the New York Mayflower Society
1991	USA Today Award for Excellence in Investment Management
1991–1996	Member of the Board of Trustees, Westminster Abbey Trust
1983–1985	Member Templeton College Council
1993	Royal Society of the Arts Benjamin Franklin Award
1993	Lifetime Achievement Award from the Layman's National Bible Association
1994	*Wall Street Week* Hall of Fame Award
1995	National Business Hall of Fame Award from the Junior Achievement Association
1997	The Abraham Lincoln Award presented by the Union League of Philadelphia
1998	Mutual Funds Lifetime Achievement Award

Colleges and Degrees

Yale University
June 1934   Bachelor of Arts

University of Oxford (Balliol College)
June 1936   M.A. (Rhodes Scholar)

Beaver College
June 1965   Honorary Doctor of Laws

Wilson College
May 1974   Honorary Doctor of Literature

Buena Vista College
May 1979   Honorary Doctor of Divinity

Marquette University
May 1980   Honorary Doctor of Laws

Maryville College
May 1984   Honorary Doctor of Laws

University of the South
May 1984   Honorary Doctor of Civil Law

Florida Southern College
February 1990   Honorary Doctor of Literature

Manhattan College
May 1990   Honorary Doctor of Literature

Babson College
May 1992   Honorary Doctor of Laws

University of Rochester
May 1992   Honorary Doctor of Laws

Rhodes College
May 1992   Honorary Doctor of Laws

University of Dubuque
September 1992   Honorary Doctor of Humane Letters

Jamestown College
May 1993   Honorary Doctor of Laws

Louisiana College
May 1993   Honorary Doctor of Laws

Campbell College
September 1993   Honorary Doctor of Humane Letters

Moravian College
May 1994   Honorary Doctor of Laws

Stonehill College
May 1995   Honorary Doctor of Philosophy

Furman University
November 1995   Honorary Doctor of Humanities

Notre Dame University
May 1996   Honorary Doctor of Laws

Methodist College of North Carolina
April 1997   Honorary Doctor of Laws

Templeton Prize Programs

£750,000	Templeton Prize for Progress in Religion
£22,000	Templeton UK Project Trust Award
$4,200 (annually)	Reporter of the Year Award (US)
SF3,500 (annually)	Templeton European Religion Writer of the Year Award
$4,200 (annually)	Templeton "Laws of Life" Essay Contest

Buildings and Scholarships

Templeton Building, Nassau
Templeton Hall, Princeton Theological Seminary
Templeton College, Oxford
Templeton Library, Sewanee, Tennessee (under construction)
Memorial Plaques, Henry VII Chapel, Westminster Abbey

John M. Templeton Scholarship Endowment Fund, Princeton
Theological Seminary (funded by the Barra Foundation)
John Templeton Scholarship, Zeta Psi Fraternity, Yale University
Templeton Scholarship, University of the South
Judith Folk Templeton Memorial Scholarship, Princeton Theological
Seminary

Books by John Marks Templeton

AUTHOR
Is Progress Speeding Up? Our Multiplying Multitudes of Blessings
This book is a thought-provoking documentation of human
progress in the last century. In spite of the pessimism that prevails

in the media, people are better fed, better clothed, better housed, and better educated than at any previous time. Loaded with statistics, charts, and photographs that illustrate this perspective, the book covers many aspects of modern life. It is a reassuring and uplifting view of the state of the world and where it is going.

Golden Nuggets
This inspiring collection of sayings by Sir John Templeton provides a welcoming book for a person seeking deeper meaning in life. Filled with practical and uplifting advice, it is based on a lifetime of experience. For young or old, rich or poor, this wisdom will find many applications in one's life.

Worldwide Laws of Life: 200 Eternal Spiritual Principles
This treasury of wisdom is drawn from major sacred scriptures of the world and various schools of philosophical thought, as well as from scientists, artists, historians, and others. Its aim is to assist people of all ages to learn more about the universal truths of life that transcend modern times or particular cultures.

Is God the Only Reality? Science Points to a Deeper Meaning of the Universe
(with Robert L. Herrmann)
Reviewing the latest findings in fields from particle physics to archaeology, the book leads the reader to see how mysterious the universe is, even to the very science that seeks to reduce it to a few simple principles. Far from concluding that religion and science are in opposition, the book shows how these two fields of inquiry are intimately linked, and how much they can offer to one another.

Discovering the Laws of Life
Two hundred "laws of life" come not only from the experiences of one of the world's most prominent businessmen, but also from the scriptures of the great spiritual traditions. This collection can serve as inspiration to the reader or form the basis for a study group.

The Templeton Plan: 21 Steps to Personal Success and Real Happiness
(as described to James Ellison)
John Templeton shares the secrets of his phenomenal success in 21 principles that provide readers with solid guidelines for prosperity and happiness. He emphasizes truthfulness, perseverance, thrift, enthusiasm, humility, and altruism—qualities that can help everyone discover and develop his or her individual abilities.

The God Who Would Be Known: Revelations of the Divine in Contemporary Science (with Robert L. Herrmann)
"This is a book about signals of transcendence," the authors write, "about points to the Infinite that are coming to us not from mystics but instead through the most recent findings of science." Positive in tone, this outstanding work seeks to preserve the mystery and wonder of our universe and emphasizes the potential blessings intended for us by God.

Riches for the Mind and Spirit
This book contains a collection of John Templeton's favorite inspirational passages from the Bible, from philosophers and poets, and from other writers.

The Humble Approach: Scientists Discover God
For generations the discoveries of science tended to challenge the very existence of God. John Templeton makes a striking argument for just the opposite point of view. He goes to the writings of many of the world's leading scientific thinkers—as diverse as Albert Einstein and Teilhard de Chardin—and discovers them in awe of the universe, perceiving the hand of Divine mystery at work.

Global Investing: The Templeton Way
(as told to Norman Berryessa and Eric Kirzner)
Readers will learn how to protect their money by following a strategy of global investing that both maximizes potential and minimizes risk factors.

EDITOR
Spiritual Evolution: Scientists Discuss Their Beliefs
(with Kenneth Seeman Giniger)
These personal essays by esteemed scientists describe their spiritual journeys. They share their experiences of reconciling scientific and religious perspectives.

How Large is God? The Voices of Scientists and Theologians
Addressing this question, these essays reveal how very little we know about God and fundamental spiritual principles. Recent scientific research has shown that the universe is staggering in size and intricacy, and some scientists are now suggesting that our concept of God is much too small.

Evidence of Purpose: Scientists Discover the Creator
In this volume, respected scientists describe new developments in their fields and the relationship with theological views of the universe.

Looking Forward: The Next Forty Years
Ten experts discuss future trends in their fields and explain why they recommend an optimistic outlook. In communications, education, the economy, and more, change is in the forecast—change for the better.

Board of Advisors of the John Templeton Foundation Humility Theology Information Center

North America

MRS. ELIZABETH PEALE ALLEN, vice chairman of the Peale Center for Christian Living in Pawling, New York, is chair of the board of the Positive Thinking Foundation.

DR. V. ELVING ANDERSON, professor emeritus of genetics and cell biology, is former director of the Dight Laboratories at the University of Minnesota. A diplomate of the American Board of Medical Genetics, his research in human genetics has explored the influence of genetics on behavior, mental retardation, and epilepsy.

PROFESSOR FRANCISCO J. AYALA, Donald Bren professor of biological sciences and professor of philosophy at the University of California, Irvine, is a member of the President's Committee of Advisors on Science and Technology and has been president and chair of the board of the American Association for the Advancement of Science and the Society for the Study of Evolution. His research focuses on population and evolutionary genetics, including the origin of species, the genetic diversity of populations, and the molecular clock of evolution.

DR. IAN G. BARBOUR, professor emeritus in physics and religion (science, technology, and society) at Carleton College in Northfield, Minnesota, and a 1989-91 Gifford Lecturer, has written several books addressing the interface of religion and science, including *Religion in an Age of Science* and *Ethics in an Age of Technology*.

DR. RONALD COLE-TURNER, H. Parker Sharp associate professor of theology and ethics at Pittsburgh Theological Seminary, is a member of the advisory board of the American Association for the Advancement of Science program of dialogue between science and religion. He is chair of the United Church of Christ working group on faith, science, and technology and chair of the task force on genetic engineering for the United Church of Christ. He has written extensively on the relationship between religion and genetics and is coauthor of the book *Pastoral Genetics: Theology*.

DR. FREEMAN DYSON, professor of physics at the Institute for Advanced Study in Princeton, a fellow of the Royal Society of London, and a 1985 Gifford Lecturer, has received numerous honors for his work in physics and ethics in science with regard to arms control. Widely published, he received the Phi Beta Kappa Award in science in 1988 for his book *Infinite in All Directions*.

DR. DIANA L. ECK, professor of comparative religion and Indian studies at Harvard University, is chair of the committee on the study of religion within the faculty of arts and sciences and a member of the faculty of divinity. Her extensive work on India includes the book *Banaras, City of Light*. In 1995, she was awarded the Henry Luce Fellowship in theology for her work on the book *Multireligious America: New Challenges for American Pluralism*.

DR. ROBERT EMMONS, professor of psychology at the University of California–Davis, received his doctorate in personality and social ecology from the University of Illinois at Urbana-Champaign. He is the author of more than sixty original publications including *The Psychology of Ultimate Concern* and is a consulting editor for the *Journal of Personality and Social Psychology* and the *International Journal for the Psychology of Religion*. His research focuses on personal goals, spirituality, and mental and physical well-being.

MR. FOSTER FRIESS, chair of Friess Associates (managers of more than $12 billion in equities), is a graduate of the University of Wisconsin. He currently serves on the advisory council of the Royal Swedish Academy of Sciences in Stockholm, which awards the Nobel Prize for chemistry and physics, as well as on the executive committee of the Council for National Policy, which networks leaders in the United States who are committed to a strong national defense, traditional values, and the free enterprise system.

DR. LINDA K. GEORGE, professor of sociology, psychology, and psychiatry at Duke University, is also associate director of the Duke University Center for the Study of Aging and Human Development and of its Center for the Study of Religion, Aging and Health. She is a past president of the Gerontological Society of America and the author of seven books and nearly 200 book chapters and journal articles. Her research interests include spirituality and health, as well as the effects of stress and social support on health.

THE REVEREND THOMAS W. GILLESPIE, president of Princeton Theological Seminary, is a member of the Presbytery of New Brunswick, the Association of Governing Boards Advisory Council of Presidents, and a trustee of the Interdenominational Theological Center in Atlanta, Georgia. He is the author of the book *The First Theologians: A Study in Early Christian Prophecy.* An alumnus of Princeton Theological Seminary, he earned his doctorate in New Testament studies from the Claremont Graduate School.

PROFESSOR OWEN J. GINGERICH, professor of astronomy and of the history of science at the Harvard-Smithsonian Center for Astrophysics in Cambridge, is a member of the American Philosophical Society, the American Academy of Arts and Sciences, and the International Academy of the History of the Sciences. He has published more than 500 technical and educational articles and reviews.

MR. KENNETH S. GINIGER, president of the K.S. Giniger Company, Inc., has published several books with Sir John Templeton that address science and religion. He is chair of the Layman's National Bible Association.

MR. PETER GRUBER, president of Globalvest Management Company, L.P., a United States-based, Securities and Exchange Commission-registered investment advisor, invests globally for private clients and is active in the securities market of Latin America and other emerging markets. He manages more than $1 billion from his headquarters in Saint Thomas, U.S. Virgin Islands, and additional offices in Rio de Janeiro.

PROFESSOR GERTRUDE HIMMELFARB, professor emeritus of history at the Graduate School of the City University of New York, is a fellow of the British Academy, the Royal Historical Society, the American Philosophical Society, the American Academy of Arts and Sciences, and the Society of American Historians. She is on the Council of Scholars of the Library of Congress, the Council of Academic Advisors of the American Enterprise Institute, and the Board of Advisors of the Library of America. Writing copiously on Victorian England and on contemporary society and culture, her most recent book is *The Demoralization of Society: From Victorian Virtues to Modern Values.*

MR. CHARLES E. JOHNSON, president and chief executive officer of Templeton Worldwide, Inc. & Franklin Institutional Services Corporation, is senior vice president and director of Franklin Resources, Inc., the parent company of the Templeton organization. He also serves as a director or officer of many of the various Franklin and Templeton mutual funds and subsidiaries. He received his master's of business administration degree from the Harvard University Graduate School of Business and is a certified public accountant.

THE REVEREND CHRISTOPHER B. KAISER, professor of historical and systematic theology at Western Theological Seminary, Holland, Michigan, has published in the field of historical studies in theology and science and the relation of science, theology, and society.

DR. HAROLD G. KOENIG, director of the program on religion, aging, and health at the Center for Aging, Duke University Medical Center, is also assistant professor of medicine and psychiatry, Division of Geriatric Medicine, Duke University Medical Center. He is also a diplomate of the American Board of Psychiatry and Neurology.

DR. DAVID B. LARSON, a psychiatrist, is a former senior fellow at the National Institute for Mental Health and is currently president of the National Institute for Healthcare Research. He has published journal articles and a psychiatric training manual demonstrating that spirituality and religious practice can benefit physical and mental health and healing.

MR. ROBERT F. LEHMAN, president and chief executive officer of the Fetzer Institute and chair of the board of the Fetzer Memorial Trust, has been vice president and director of international programs at the Kettering Foundation and director of the exploratory fund sponsoring research on the relationship of consciousness to health and education.

DR. MARTIN E. MARTY, senior scholar at the Park Ridge Center for the Study of Health, Faith and Ethics in Chicago, is the editor of *Second Opinion*, a journal providing a forum for the interface of health, faith, and ethics. Director of the Public Religion Project and Fairfax M. Cone distinguished service professor emeritus, University of Chicago Divinity School, he contributed the opening chapter of the recently published book *Dimensions of Forgiveness: Psychological Research & Theological Perspectives*.

DR. DALE A. MATTHEWS, associate professor of medicine at Georgetown University School of Medicine and senior fellow at the National Institute for Healthcare Research, practices and teaches general internal medicine. He also conducts research on the doctor-patient relationship, patient satisfaction with medical care, chronic fatigue syndrome, and the psychological and spiritual dimensions of medicine.

MR. GARY D. MOORE, with twenty years of Wall Street experience, including service as senior vice president of investments for Paine-Webber, founded Gary Moore & Co. to provide counsel to ethical and religious investors. He hosts a syndicated radio commentary program, "The Spirit of Money," and is the author of several books integrating spirituality and wealth management, including *The Christian Guide to Wise Investing; Ten Golden Rules for Financial Success: Riches I've Gathered from Legendary Mutual Fund Manager Sir John M. Templeton;* and the recently published *Spiritual Investments: Wall Street Wisdom from the Career of Sir John Templeton.*

DR. DAVID G. MYERS, John Dirk Werkman professor of psychology at Hope College, Holland, Michigan, has published ten books and two best-selling psychology textbooks. He is the recipient of the Gordon Allport Prize for his National Science Foundation-funded experiments on group influence. His most recent publication is *The Pursuit of Happiness: Who is Happy—and Why.* He is also a trustee of the John Templeton Foundation.

DR. SEYYED HOSSEIN NASR, university professor of Islamic studies at George Washington University in Washington, D.C., was the first Muslim to give the Gifford Lectures in 1981. He is the author of numerous books and over 200 articles; has lectured extensively throughout the Islamic world, Western Europe, North and Central America, India, Japan, and Australia; and has participated in numerous conferences and congresses on Islam, philosophy, comparative religion, and the environmental crisis.

DR. STEPHEN G. POST, professor of biomedical ethics at the School of Medicine, Case Western Reserve University, Cleveland, serves on the National Ethics Advisory Panel of the Alzheimer's Disease and Related Disorders Association and is ethics editor for *Alzheimer's Disease and Associated Disorders.* He received his doctorate in religious ethics and moral philosophy from the University of Chicago Divinity School. In 1998, he received the annual award for outstanding public service from the Alzheimer's Association. His most recent book is *The Moral Challenge of Alzheimer's Disease.*

DR. V. S. RAMACHANDRAN, director of the Center for Brain and Cognition, University of California–San Diego, holds academic positions at both the Salk Institute and the University of California–San Diego and has published and lectured internationally on visual neuroscience. Among his achievements is his appointment as editor-in-chief of the four-volume *Encyclopedia of Human Behavior.*

MR. LAURANCE S. ROCKEFELLER, philanthropist, business executive, and conservationist, has held various chairs and trustee appointments for a number of national, academic, and humanitarian organizations. He has been the recipient of many awards and medals for his conservation work and philanthropic interests, including the Congressional Gold Medal in 1991.

DR. ALLAN SANDAGE, graduate of the University of Illinois, received his doctorate in astronomy from the California Institute of Technology. He began his career at Mount Wilson Observatory, where he was chosen by Edgar Hubble to work as his personal assistant. He is recognized for his work in stellar evolution, the composition of galaxies, and observational high-energy astrophysics and is best known in observational cosmology, measuring the rate of expansion and age of the universe. A recipient of numerous awards including the Presidential Medal of Science and the American Astronomical Society's Russell Prize, he was a 1986–87 visiting professor at Johns Hopkins University in the department of physics and astronomy and senior visiting fellow at the Space Telescope Science Institute.

DR. LAWRENCE E. SULLIVAN, director of the Harvard University Center for the Study of World Religions, professor of religion, past president of the American Academy of Religions, and deputy secretary-general of the International Association for the History of Religions, has received numerous awards, including a Henry Luce Fellowship. Author of many articles and editor of several books, he received the American Council of Learned Societies Book Award for Best First Book and the Award for Best Book in Philosophy and Religion given by the Association of American Publishers for *Icanchu's Drum: An Orientation to Meaning in South American Religions*.

DR. CHARLES H. TOWNES, professor in the graduate school at the University of California–Berkeley and a Nobel Prize recipient in physics, has published many articles on science and theology. His research was primarily responsible for the development of the laser.

DR. HOWARD VAN TILL, professor and chairman of the department of physics at Calvin College, Michigan, is a member of the American Astronomical Society and the American Scientific Affiliation. He has written books and articles addressing creation and cosmology from a Christian perspective.

DR. EVERETT L. WORTHINGTON, JR. , professor of psychology at Virginia Commonwealth University and director of VCU's Counseling Psychology program, published an extensive review of research on religion in counseling in 1986 and recently provided a ten-year update to this review in *Psychological Bulletin*. Within his specialty of marriage and family counseling, he edits a professional journal, has published numerous books and articles in peer-reviewed journals and in popular magazines, and has given extensive professional presentations and workshops on marital therapy, marital enrichment, and forgiveness. The director of the Campaign for Forgiveness Research based in Richmond, Virginia, which supports interdisciplinary scientific inquiry and dialogue on forgiveness, he also is the editor of *Dimensions of Forgiveness: Psychological Research & Theological Perspectives.*

International

DR. M. A. Zaki Badawi, principal of the Muslim College in London, is chair of the United Kingdom Imams and Mosques Council and the United Kingdom Muslim Law (Shariah) Council. He is a lecturer at Al-Azhar University, Cairo, and frequently writes and broadcasts on Muslim affairs.

PROFESSOR R. J. BERRY, professor of genetics at University College, London, was previously the chair of several ecological organizations and the Research Scientists Christian Fellowship (now Christians in Science). He is currently chair of the Environmental Issues Network of CCBI and has lectured and published extensively with regard to the preservation of the environment.

DR. GEORGE F. R. ELLIS, who has been a visiting lecturer and professor in cosmology, physics, and astronomy across the globe, including South Africa, England, Germany, Canada, Italy, and the United States, received his doctorate in applied mathematics and theoretical physics from Saint John's College, Cambridge University. He is a fellow of the Royal Society of South Africa and was president of the International Society of Relativity and Gravitation. He coauthored the book *On the Moral Nature of the Universe: Theology, Cosmology, and Ethics (Theology and the Sciences)* with former foundation advisor Nancey Murphy and collaborated with Stephen Hawking on several publications, including *The Large-Scale Structure of Space-Time.*

DR. BRUNO GUIDERDONI, astrophysicist at the French National Center for Scientific Research, is a researcher at the Paris Institute of Astrophysics focusing on galaxy formation. Since 1993, he has been in charge of the weekly TV program *Knowing Islam* in France. In his papers and lectures, he presents the intellectual and spiritual aspects of Islam, reflects on the relation between science and the Islamic tradition, and promotes an interreligious dialogue.

DR. PETER E. HODGSON, head of the nuclear physics theoretical group at Oxford University and senior research fellow at Corpus Christi College, has published widely on the future direction of nuclear energy applications, as well as in the area of Christianity and science.

PROFESSOR MALCOLM JEEVES, research professor of psychology, University of Saint Andrews, is president of the Royal Society of Edinburgh and was made Commander of the Order of the British Empire in the Queen's National New Year's Honours in 1992 for his service to science and psychology. He established the department of psychology at Saint Andrews University, where his research interests center around cognitive psychology and neuropsychology.

THE REVEREND DR. ARTHUR R. PEACOCKE, warden emeritus of the Society of Ordained Scientists and Honorable Chaplain of Christ Church Cathedral, Oxford University, is also the director of the Ian Ramsey Centre there. His primary discipline is the physical chemistry of biological systems, and he has been the recipient of the Le Compte DuNuoy Prize. A 1993 Gifford Lecturer, his religion and science writings include his recent book *Theology for a Science Age*.

SIR JOHN C. POLKINGHORNE, president of Queen's College, Cambridge University, is a member of the Church of England Doctrine Committee and General Synod. Former professor of applied physics at Cambridge, he has published many papers on theoretical elementary particle physics, and among his science and religion books are *Science and Creation* and *Reason and Reality*.

PROFESSOR F. RUSSELL STANNARD, currently vice president of the Institute of Physics and professor and department head of physics at the Open University in the United Kingdom, has served on the Prime Minister's Advisory Committee on Science and Technology. He has authored the popular "Uncle Albert" series of books introducing physics to children and is the author of *Grounds for Reasonable Belief*, the twelfth book in the *Theology and Science* series. He is a trustee of the John Templeton Foundation.

PROFESSOR KEITH WARD, regius professor of divinity at the University of Oxford University and former professor of history and the philosophy of religion at King's College, London University, is one of the country's foremost writers on comparative religion and Christian issues. A Gifford Lecturer, his most recent book, *Defending the Soul*, is an affirmation of human divinity and value.

Sir Sigmund Sternberg
Ms. Renee Dawn Stirling
Mr. Christopher Templeton
Mr. Handly Templeton
Mr. Harvey M. Templeton, Jr.
Mr. Harvey M. Templeton, III
Miss Heather E. Templeton
Miss Jennifer A. Templeton
Mrs. Jewel Templeton
Sir John M. Templeton
Dr. John M. Templeton, Jr.
Dr. Josephine Templeton
Miss Lauren Templeton
Mrs. Rebecca L. Templeton
Mrs. Rebecca M. Templeton

The Reverend Professor Thomas
  F. Torrance
Miss Elizabeth Transou
Mr. Stamps Transou
Professor Dr. Carl Friedrich von
  Weizsäcker
Ms. Mary P. Walker
Mr. Linford G. Williams
Dr. Anne D. Zimmerman
Dr. Gail Zimmerman
Mr. Michael D. Zimmerman
Mr. Mitchell Dean Zimmerman
Ms. Rhonda Sue Zimmerman-
  Durdahl

Recipients of the
Templeton Prize for Progress in Religion

1973   Mother Teresa of Calcutta, founder of the Missionaries of Charity. She saw Christ in the "poorest of the poor" in what has become a worldwide ministry to the dying.

1974   Brother Roger, founder and prior of the Taize Community in France. Taize communes have appeared all over the world, bridging the gap between many denominations and languages.

1975   Sir Sarvepalli Radhakrishnan, who was president of India and an Oxford professor of Eastern religions and ethics. A strong proponent of religious idealism as the most hopeful political instrument for peace.

1976   H.E. Leon Joseph Cardinal Suenens, who was archbishop of Malines-Brussels. A pioneer of the charismatic renewal and a strong proponent of Christian unity.

1977   Chiara Lubich, founder of the Focolare Movement in Italy, which has become a worldwide network of more than a million people in communes and private homes engaged in spiritual renewal and ecumenism.

1978   The Very Rev. Professor Thomas F. Torrance, who was moderator of the Church of Scotland. A leader in the new understanding of the convergence of theology and science.

1979   Rev. Nikkyo Niwano, founder of Rissho Kosei-Kai and the World Conference on Religion and Peace, Kyoto, Japan. A Buddhist world leader in efforts toward peace and understanding among religious groups.

1980   Professor Ralph Wendell Burhoe, founder and former editor of *Zygon: Journal of Religion and Science,* U.S.A. A leading advocate of an intellectually credible synthesis of the religious and scientific traditions.

1981   Dame Cicely Saunders, originator of the modern hospice movement, England. Pioneer in the care of the terminally ill by emphasizing spiritual growth and modern methods of pain management.

1982   Rev. Dr. Billy Graham, founder of the Billy Graham Evangelistic Association, U.S.A. He has preached the Christian gospel in more than fifty countries, brought diverse denominations together, and promoted respect for all peoples.

1983 Mr. Aleksandr Solzhenitsyn, U.S.A. Historical writer and novelist who has been an outspoken critic of totalitarianism and a strong proponent of spiritual awakening in the democracies as well.

1984 Rev. Michael Bourdeaux, founder of Keston College, England, a research center for the study of religion in communist countries. He has been a fearless supporter of Christians in Russia.

1985 Sir Alister Hardy, who was founder of the Sir Alister Hardy Research Center at Oxford, England. An outstanding biologist, he also had a deep interest in man's spiritual nature. His work has demonstrated widespread religious experience in the British Isles.

1986 Rev. Dr. James McCord, who was chancellor of the Center of Theological Inquiry, Princeton, U.S.A. A leader in spiritual education as president of Princeton Theological Seminary.

1987 Rev. Stanley L. Jaki, professor of history and philosophy of science at Seton Hall University, U.S.A. His reinterpretation of the history of science provides a context for renewed belief in God in a scientific age.

1988 Dr. Inamullah Khan, secretary general of the World Muslim Congress, Karachi, Pakistan. Proponent of peace within and between the world's religions.

1989 The Very Reverend Lord MacLeod of the Iona Community, Scotland. A leader for spiritual renewal in the Church of Scotland.
     Jointly with
     Professor Carl Friedrich von Weizsäcker of Starnberg, West Germany. Physicist and philosopher, a strong voice for dialogue between science and theology.

1990 Baba Amte, India. A learned Hindu scholar and philanthropist who has relieved the poverty of millions in rural India.
     Jointly with
     Professor Charles Birch, Sydney, Australia. Molecular biologist and strong proponent of process theology and environmental stewardship.

1991 The Right Honourable Lord Jakobovits, London. The chief rabbi of Britain, a leader in Jewish concern for medicine and especially medical ethics.

1992   Rev. Dr. Kyung-Chik Han, Korea. Pioneer in helping the Presbyterian Church in Korea to become in only thirty years the largest Presbyterian denomination on earth.

1993   Charles Wendell Colson, founder of Prison Fellowship. A strong Christian force for change in the American prison system.

1994   Michael Novak, historical and theological scholar at the American Enterprise Institute for Public Policy. A powerful voice for re-emphasis of our rich religious and philosophical traditions.

1995   Dr. Paul C. Davies, currently professor of natural philosophy at the University of Adelaide in Australia. He is a leading authority in expounding the idea of purpose in the universe and author of more than twenty books.

1996   Dr. William R. Bright, president and founder of Campus Crusade for Christ International.

1997   Pandurang Shastri Athavale, founder and leader of a spiritual self-knowledge movement in India that has liberated millions from the shackles of poverty and moral dissipation.

1998   Sir Sigmund Sternberg has become an "interfaith ambassador," working to resolve conflicts within and between religions. He helped make the first papal visit to a synagogue possible.

APPENDIX E

Examples of Grants
from the John Templeton Foundation

The John Templeton Foundation believes a path of cooperation between the sciences and all religions will lead humanity to a deeper understanding of the universe, the unlimited creative spirit behind it, and our place in it. The Foundation's spiritual information through science programs include the following awards.

American Association for the Advancement of Science (AAAS), Washington, D. C. Project Director: Dr. Audrey Chapman. Program on Dialogue between Science and Religion. The grant provides a five-year funding commitment to help establish a science and religion dialogue under the direction of the Directorate for Science and Policy Programs at AAAS.

American Scientific Affiliation, Ipswich, Massachusetts. Project Director: Donald Munro Ph.D. The Templeton/ASA 1996–1997 Lecture Series involved presentations at fourteen science-religion course–winning colleges and universities in the United States. Thirty-two lectures took place during the 1996–97 school year.

Association of Unity Churches, Lee's Summit, Missouri.
• Project Manager: Ms. Linda Harbin. The grant provides funds to operate a radio/media program that offers consultation, education, and products to all Unity Ministry radio programs.
• Project Manager: Ms. Barbara O'Hearne. Unity Church Development and Management Consultation enables consultants to provide training, workshops, and general consultation to churches, ministers, and boards worldwide.
• Project Manager: Ms. Barbara O'Hearne. Unity Church Development and Management Consultation. Funds provided for on-site efforts at individual Unity Ministries to facilitate minister/board development, strategic planning, and general ministry administration.

Calvin College, Grand Rapids, Michigan. Project Director: Dr. Howard Van Till. The "Templeton Awards for Exemplary Papers in Humility Theology"is a continuation of the "Call for Papers in Humility Theology" program that awards authors for, and encourages scholarly research into, the constructive interaction of: 1) theology and the natural sciences; 2) religion and the medical sciences; and 3) religion and the human behavioral sciences.

Center for Theology and the Natural Sciences, Berkeley, California.
- Project Director: Dr. Ted Peters. Funds to support the Templeton Foundation University Lectures. Series theme is "Nature and God: Spiritual Knowledge Through the Lens of Science." Series will be offered at a number of large university campuses. Select lectures will be offered on smaller campuses, including more teaching-oriented colleges.
- Project Director: Dr. Robert Russell. A conference series called "Science and the Spiritual Quest." Major interdisciplinary conference and workshop series explores the spiritual and religious impact of the new scientific perspective on the universe.
- Project Director: Dr. Robert Russell. "Prize Competition for Outstanding Books in Theology and the Natural Sciences." A competition for books on the theological and/or spiritual dimensions of the natural sciences. Both conference-edited and single-author books will be judged.

Duke University Medical Center, Durham, North Carolina.
- Principal Investigator: Harold Koenig, M.D. For a project titled "Do Religious People Live Longer?" Utilizing previously funded data sets that include religious variables and mortality outcomes, the researchers will more carefully examine the relationship between religion and survival.
- Center for the Study of Religion/Spirituality and Health. Expansion over four-year period of the Medical Center's activities through a research initiative designed to provide the Center with core resources and infrastructure support. The Center will increase scientific research on spirituality and health/religion at Duke and at other institutions and increase the number of peer-reviewed publications coming out of the Center. The Center will also work to expand its federal, foundation, private sector, and industry support.

Fuller Theological Seminary, Pasadena, California. Project Director: Dr. Nancey Murphy. Conference series and book publication, *Portraits of Human Nature*, will investigate the nature of the human person. A group of eleven scholars will contribute, each offering a perspective from their respective disciplines—biblical studies, theology, philosophy, ethics, human sciences, and the natural sciences.

Georgetown University, Washington, D. C. Principal Investigator: Dr. John Haught. International Study Conference on Science and Religion entitled "Science, Cosmology and Teleology: Intercultural and Multi-disciplinary Perspectives." A matching award supported this international symposium on the intercultural dimensions of science and religion at the 1997 AAAS Annual Meeting in Seattle, Washington.

Gordon College, Wenham, Massachusetts. Program Director: Dr. Robert Herrmann.
- Science & Religion Course Program
  Eight international workshops and an awards competition for up to one hundred colleges, universities, and schools of theology, with the goal of encouraging the development and continuation of science and religion courses within the college level curriculum. Program includes a regional outreach organized by each workshop site in order to increase the awareness of the science and religion dialogue within the academic community.
- *Progress in Theology* newsletter
  The newsletter promotes an increased awareness of projects undertaken by the John Templeton Foundation.
- Science & Religion Course Program Development Grant
  This development grant offers further support to Science & Religion Course Winners to continue to develop their award-winning programs. An additional goal of this program is to allow past winners to attend additional workshops.
- University and College Student Essay Contest on Humility Theology
  Prizes to students and faculty mentors of award-winning courses for best essays on subjects centering on humility theology.
- German Science & Religion Conferences
  To attract German faculty and doctoral students to the field of science and religion, a conference was conducted to explore topics, common interests, experiences in course work, and future research plans. A second interdisciplinary conference took place in Summer 1998 to further develop research and course work in Europe.

Institute of Religion in an Age of Science, Inc., St. Louis, Missouri.
- Project Director: Dr. Ursula Goodenough. Award for two Star Island Lectureships, one North American lecturer and one international lecturer at the Star Island Conference, the annual meeting for members and guests of the Institute.

- Project Director: Professor Kevin Sharpe. *Science & Spirit* newsletter. Financial support toward operating expenses for print and electronic publication. The newsletter provides commentary and review of events, symposia, presentations, associated organizations, and books and publications that are representative of the dialogue between the scientific and religious communities.

Mind/Body Medical Institute, Boston, Massachusetts. Project Director: Herbert Benson, M.D.
- Funding for a course titled "Spirituality and Healing in Medicine," offered through the Harvard Medical School's Department of Continuing Education. This course explores the relationship between spirituality and healing in medicine and gives perspectives from world religions. This course was offered in Boston and Houston between 1996 and 1998.
- Contents of special edition of *Mind/Body Medicine Journal* derived from presentations made at the Lansdowne Conferences on Spirituality and Health, hosted by the National Institute for Healthcare Research.

National Institute for Healthcare Research, Rockville, Maryland: Project Director: David Larson, M.D.
- *Faith and Medicine Connection* Newsletter
  This newsletter deals with issues of the integration of religion, spirituality, and medicine. It allows researchers, deans, professors, medical students, and other key professionals to stay better informed about current research, education, and training developments in the interface between medical science and religion.
- Psychiatry Residency Training
  A program encouraging use of "Model Curriculum for Psychiatry Residency Training" to enhance recognition of the importance of spiritual issues.
- 1998 Medical Education Conference
  Conference on integrating spirituality into medical school curricular development. Eight NIHR-selected presenters taught participants how to accomplish this integration and sustain such education and training efforts once they are in place. Small group discussions encouraged courses on medicine and spirituality. Ten Faith and Medicine Curricular Award winners were invited.
- Faith and Medicine Curricular Awards Program
  Third year of a program is designed to expand the scope of medical education by encouraging model medical school courses

which address the important, but long-neglected, domains of religion and spirituality in medical care.

- Medical Education Opinion-Leaders conference series
  Three working meetings, beginning in fall 1997 and held in Washington, D.C., were designed to build on the progress made at the April 1997 conference on curricular development and assisted in developing an even more critical 1998 conference on spiritual education in clinical care. The conferences were attended by twelve invitees who are national medial opinion leaders.
- Scientific Progress in Spiritual Research Conference Series
  Three conferences (July 1996, and January and July 1997) explored the scientific investigation of religious and spiritual factors in four clinical research areas: Physical illness, mental illness, addiction, and the link between neurobiological assessment and spiritual life. Existing barriers to spiritual research in each clinical area were examined, and goals and objectives were set to overcome these barriers.

Prison Fellowship, Washington, D. C. Project Director: Dr. Karen Strong. "Research on Family and Religion—Systematic Reviews of Family and Religion Literature." Dr. Strong will complete two systematic reviews on family factors already started in the "juvenile delinquency" and "adult criminality" literatures. Two systematic reviews on religious factors will also be initiated and completed. Reanalysis of the data from two previous studies, the New York State Prison Fellowship Study and the Rutgers University Study, will assist in this project.

St. George's House, Windsor Castle, Windsor, UK. Project Director: Mr. Dominick Harrod. The Templeton United Kingdom Project Trust Award is designed to encourage original entrepreneurship in religion. Two awards of £3,000 are presented semi-annually to both an individual and an organization.

University of Syracuse, Syracuse, New York. Project Director: Rev. Dr. George Koch. "In Whose Cosmos" Conference was a major science and religion conference August 11–17, 1997, for those interested in the faith-and-science dialogue, especially clergy, lay leaders of churches and synagogues located in scientific communities, working scientists, and science teachers.

Virginia Commonwealth University, Richmond, Virginia. Principal Investigator: Rev. Dr. Lindon Eaves.

- "Family Spiritual Values in the Transition from Adolescence to Young Adulthood," a project that analyzes the protective role of family spiritual values in the healthy transition from adolescence to young adulthood. The study focuses on the interaction between genetic risk and environmental protection in the use and abuse of alcohol.
- "Religion, Values, and Health: Unraveling the Role of Genes and Environment." Three project components (analysis, workshop, and book) will improve collaboration among scientists conducting family studies on the role of religion in health-promoting values. These peer-reviewed articles will be published in a landmark book. The workshop will be conducted under the direction of the Center for Theology and the Natural Sciences.
- "The Effects of Parental Religion on Adolescent Mental Health and Substance Abuse," a project to examine the interaction of family religious affiliation and practice with other genetic and social factors using the "Virginia Twin Study of Adolescent Behavioral Development."

Zygon: Journal of Religion and Science, Chicago, Illinois. Project Director: Philip Hefner, Chicago Center for Religion and Science. Ongoing support for a new section of *Zygon,* the Teacher's File, which provides accessible materials and peer support for teachers of science and religion courses in colleges, universities, and seminaries.

Character Development

Recognizing the importance of personal moral values to society, the John Templeton Foundation supports programs that advocate character and spiritual development. The Foundation's character development programs include the following awards.

American Textbook Council, New York, New York. Project Director: Mr. Gilbert Sewall. Funds to conduct project titled "Religion and Moral Education in Schools." Project consists of a national symposium on religion and moral education and production of a guide for school districts, teachers, curriculum writers, and state education officials, which will provide information on how religion can be incorporated into moral education materials designed for public schools.

Association of Unity Churches, Lee's Summit, Missouri. Project Director: Rev. Shay St. John. "Caring Now! A Living Curriculum" has been given a matching grant that will allow Unity to provide quality educational resource materials to its youth education and youth of Unity programs.

Center for Jewish and Christian Values, Washington, D. C. Project Director: Mr. Chris Gersten. "An Action Plan to Restore Faith, Religion, and Spirituality to the Schools" will be developed with the production of two complimentary sets of guidelines, one to be released by the American Textbook Council (ATC) and sponsored by the Templeton Foundation, in early 1997, and the other by the Parent-Teacher Association (PTA), outlining ways in which public schools may include religious discussions in the classroom.

Christian Education Movement, Derby, UK. Project Director: Rev. Dr. Stephen Orchard. A revised version of Sir John Templeton's "Discovering the Laws of Life," adapted for classroom use with an accompanying teacher's guide, will be published for use in UK schools.

Christian Educators Association, International, Pasadena, California. Program Director: Mr. Forrest Turpin. "Consultation for Public Education: A National Conference" is designed to bring together approximately forty Christian leaders in the field of education to produce and disseminate action plans designed to increase proactive strategies for the teaching of moral character and ethical behavior in public schools.

Florida State University, Tallahassee, Florida. Project Director: Mr. Jon Dalton, Ph.D. Cosponsorship of the Institute on College Student Values annual conference in February 1997, and partial support for the attendance of a representative from each school named to the Honor Roll for Character-Building Colleges.

The "Laws of Life" essay contest for students in Franklin County, Tennessee, has been ongoing since 1986. Each contest consists of at least thirteen awards. This is the flagship project for the formation of other "Laws of Life" essay contests being established throughout the country. The contest is conducted biannually.

Peale Center for Christian Living, Pawling, New York. Project Director: Mr. Eric Fellman. Twice yearly, *PLUS Magazine* will conduct a "Discovering the Laws of Life" essay contest to encourage young readers to reflect upon moral principals that influence their life.

Free Enterprise Education

The John Templeton Foundation seeks to encourage a greater appreciation of the importance of the free enterprise system and the values that enable it to flourish. The Foundation's free enterprise education programs include the following awards.

Colorado Council on Economic Education, Denver, Colorado. Program Director: Mrs. LaKay Schmidt. The 1996 and 1997 Templeton Lectures constituted the CCEE's annual lecture series, which attracts internationally recognized speakers. This challenge grant allows Michael Novak to serve as the guest speaker for the two Templeton Lectures.

Economic Education for Clergy, Inc., Indianapolis, Indiana. Project Director: Ms. Donna Dial, Ph.D. Support of economic and ethics courses utilizing the Templeton internship/mentoring model at the following five schools: Graduate Theological Union (Berkeley, California), Trinity Theological Seminary (Columbus, Ohio), Christian Theological Seminary (Indianapolis, Indiana), Lutheran Theological Seminary (Gettysburg, Pennsylvania), and Vanderbilt Divinity School (Nashville, Tennessee). The courses were developed for academic year 1997–98.

OPPORTUNITY International, Oak Brook, Illinois. A free enterprise endeavor that will allow for the empowerment of underprivileged individuals in Russia by providing them small loans and basic business training.

Intercollegiate Studies Institute, Wilmington, Delaware. Project Director: Mr. Gregory Wolfe. The "Honor Rolls for Education in a Free Society" consist of four separate categories featuring colleges and universities, professors, departments and programs, and textbooks. There is also a lifetime achievement award and an Outstanding Book of the Year award. The program, to be conducted every five years, is administered by Intercollegiate Studies Institute and managed directly by Mr. William Simon of the John M. Olin Foundation in New York City. The 1996 Honor Roll recipients were announced in January 1997.

1999 Science & Religion Course Competition and Workshops

The Center for Theology and the Natural Sciences

presents

1999 SCIENCE & RELIGION
COURSE COMPETITION AND WORKSHOPS

The Center for Theology and the Natural Sciences announces the 1999 Science & Religion Course Program, which includes a course competition granting awards for outstanding courses in science and religion, and a series of workshops on science and religion, course development, and pedagogy. Funded by the John Templeton Foundation, the program will award up to 100 prizes for outstanding science and religion course proposals in colleges, universities, and seminaries. Each prize includes an award of US $10,000, to be divided evenly between the course instructor and the host institution. The preliminary application deadline for applicants is *December 1, 1998*, except for those applicants attending a winter workshop.

WINTER 1999 INTRODUCTORY WORKSHOPS		SUMMER 1999 ADVANCED WORKSHOPS	
Tallahassee, Florida	January 5–10	Berkeley, California	June 4–9
Berkeley, California	January 7–12	Chicago, Illinois	June 18–23
Oxford, England	January 8–13	Boston, Massachusetts	June 28–July 2
		Oxford, England	July 8–13
		Toronto, Canada	July 8–13

*For more information on current and past programs, including details
on regional activities, please visit the Templeton Foundation web site at:*
www.templeton.org
*For 1999 program information and application materials
or workshop registration forms, please contact CTNS at:*
Peter M.J. Hess, Ph.D., Competition Coordinator
Center for Theology and the Natural Sciences ▪ 2400 Ridge Road ▪ Berkeley, CA 94709
Phone: 510.665.8141 ▪ Fax: 510.665.1589 ▪ Email:SRcourse@ctns.org ▪ www.ctns.org

This program funded by the
JOHN TEMPLETON FOUNDATION

1999 Call for Exemplary Papers in Humility Theology

JOHN TEMPLETON FOUNDATION

1999

CALL FOR EXEMPLARY PAPERS IN HUMILITY THEOLOGY

To encourage scholarly research on matters of both spiritual and scientific significance, the John Templeton Foundation invites scholars to submit published papers on topics regarding the constructive interaction of:

- Theology and the natural sciences
- Religion and the medical sciences, or
- Religion and the behavioral sciences.

These papers must proceed from professional scholarship and display a spirit of intellectual humility, a respect for varied theological traditions, and an attitude of open-minded inquiry into the varied ways in which theology/religion and the empirical sciences can be mutually informative. Papers must have been published or accepted for publication in a peer-reviewed journal or similarly selective scholarly publication, be between 3,000 and 10,000 words in length, and be accompanied by a 600-word précis (in English, even if the paper is not).

Prizes ranging from $500 to $3000 will be awarded in November 1999.
The deadline for submission of papers is June 1, 1999.

For full details and application forms, please visit our web site, or write to:
Exemplary Papers Program Director
JOHN TEMPLETON FOUNDATION
P.O. Box 8322 ▪ Radnor, Pennsylvania 19087-8322 USA
www.templeton.org

Reference: PIT

Two Hundred Spiritual Principles
from Worldwide Laws of Life

by John Marks Templeton

WEEK ONE

1 *When you rule your mind, you rule your world*—Bill Provost
2 *Where there is no vision, the people perish*—Proverbs 29:18
3 *Love has the patience to endure the fault we cannot cure*—J. Jelinek
4 *There are more possibilities in the universe than one can imagine* —Anonymous
5 *As you give, so shall you receive*—The Golden Rule (Matthew 7:12 and Luke 6:31)

WEEK TWO

1 *Your life becomes what you think*—Marcus Aurelius
2 *Love given is love received*—John M. Templeton
3 *To be forgiven, one must first forgive*—John M. Templeton
4 *An attitude of gratitude creates blessings*—John M. Templeton
5 *You fear what you do not understand*—Anonymous

WEEK THREE

1 *Nothing can bring you peace but yourself*—Ralph Waldo Emerson
2 *Listen to learn*—Alcoholics Anonymous
3 *Wisdom is born of mistakes; confront error and learn*—J. Jelinek
4 *Humility leads to prayer as well as progress and brings you in tune with the Infinite*—John M. Templeton
5 *Failing to plan is planning to fail*—Ben Franklin

WEEK FOUR

1 *Beautiful thoughts build a beautiful soul*—John M. Templeton
2 *Progress depends on diligence and perseverance* —John M. Templeton
3 *Love thy neighbor as thyself*—Matthew 19:19
4 *To be wronged is nothing unless you continue to remember it* —Confucius
5 *Enthusiasm facilitates achievement*—John M. Templeton

WEEK FIVE

1 *By giving you grow*—John M. Templeton
2 *Lost time is never found again*—Ben Franklin
3 *The family that prays together stays together*—Common Saying
4 *If at first you don't succeed; try, try again*
  —William Edward Hickson
5 *It is better to light a single candle than to curse the darkness*
  —Motto of the Christophers

WEEK SIX

1 *It is better to love than be loved*—St. Francis
2 *Thanksgiving leads to having more to give thanks for*
  —John M. Templeton
3 *You cannot be lonely if you help the lonely*—John M. Templeton
4 *You are sought after if you reflect love, joy, peace, patience, kindness, goodness, faithfulness, gentleness, and self-control*
  —John M. Templeton
5 *A smile breeds a smile*—Ted Engstrom

WEEK SEVEN

1 *Great heroes are humble*—John M. Templeton
2 Agape *given grows,* agape *hoarded dwindles*—John M. Templeton
3 *A measure of mental health is the disposition to find good everywhere*
  —John M. Templeton
4 *What the mind can conceive, it may achieve*—Anonymous
5 *By prayer you receive spiritual energy*—John M. Templeton

WEEK EIGHT

1 *What appears to us as the impossible may simply be the untried*
  —Seyyed Hossein Nasr
2 *I shall allow no man to belittle my soul by making me hate him*
  —Booker T. Washington
3 *Real success means not to remain satisfied with any limited goal*
  —Seyyed Hossein Nasr
4 *Enthusiasm is contagious*—John M. Templeton
5 *Small attempts completed will complete any undertaking*
  —Og Mandino

WEEK NINE

1 *Defeat isn't bitter if you don't swallow it*—Ted Engstrom
2 *The unexamined life is not worth living*—Socrates
3 *You are only as good as your word*—John M. Templeton

4   *Tithing often brings prosperity and honor*—John M. Templeton
5   *Self-control wins the race*—Anonymous

WEEK TEN
1   *Freedom is a fact of life*—Anonymous
2   *By asserting our will, many a closed door will open before us*
    —Seyyed Hossein Nasr
3   *Count your blessings and you will have an attitude of gratitude*
    —John M. Templeton
4   *We learn more by welcoming criticism than by rendering judgment*
    —J. Jelinek
5   *Ask not what you can expect of life; ask what life expects from you*
    —Viktor Frankel

WEEK ELEVEN
1   *You find what you look for: good or evil, problems or solutions*
    —John M. Templeton
2   *Every ending is a new beginning*—Susan Hayward
3   *The only way to have a friend is to be a friend*
    —Ralph Waldo Emerson
4   *Man is what he believes*—Anton Chekhov
5   *Our quantity of spiritual knowledge is smaller than Ptolemy's knowl-
    edge of astronomy*—John M. Templeton

WEEK TWELVE
1   *Helpfulness, not willfulness, brings rewards*—Anonymous
2   *Birds of a feather flock together*—Robert Burton
3   *Crime doesn't pay*—Anonymous
4   *You can make opposition work for you*—Anonymous
5   *No one knows what he can do until he tries*—Publilius Syrus

WEEK THIRTEEN
1   *'Tis the part of the wise man to keep himself today for tomorrow, and
    not venture all his eggs in one basket*—Miguel de Cervantes
2   *Thoughts are things*—Charles Fillmore
3   *As within, so without*—Hermetic Principle
4   *Thanksgiving, not complaining, attracts people to you*
    —John M. Templeton
5   *Perseverance makes the difference between success and defeat*
    —Anonymous

WEEK FOURTEEN

1 *The secret of a productive life can be sought and found*
   —John M. Templeton
2 *Happiness is always a by-product*—John M. Templeton
3 *The way to mend the bad world is to create the right world*
   —Ralph Waldo Emerson
4 *It is better to praise than to criticize*—John M. Templeton
5 *Laughter is the best medicine*—Norman Cousins

WEEK FIFTEEN

1 *Humility, like darkness, reveals the heavenly light*
   —Henry David Thoreau
2 *Use wisely your power of choice*—Og Mandino
3 *If you do not know what you want to achieve with your life, you may not achieve much*—John M. Templeton
4 *More is wrought by prayer than this world dreams of*
   —Alfred Lord Tennyson
5 *Everything and everyone around you is your teacher*—Ken Keyes

WEEK SIXTEEN

1 *Hitch your wagon to a star!*—Ralph Waldo Emerson
2 *The price of greatness is responsibility*—Winston Churchill
3 *Good words are worth much and cost little*—George Herbert
4 *You can never solve a problem on the same level as the problem*
   —Emmet Fox
5 *Happy relationships depend not on finding the right person, but on being the right person*—Eric Butterworth

WEEK SEVENTEEN

1 *We receive freely when we give freely*—Anonymous
2 *The truth will make you free*—John 8:32
3 *If you would find gold, you must search where gold is*
   —William Juneau
4 *Habit is the best of servants, the worst of masters*—J. Jelinek
5 *You cannot discover new oceans until you have the courage to lose sight of the shore*—Anonymous

WEEK EIGHTEEN

1 *No one's education is ever complete*—John M. Templeton
2 *Accentuate the positive; eliminate the negative*—Johnny Mercer
3 *Forgiving uplifts the forgiver*—John M. Templeton

4   *The light of understanding dissolves the phantoms of fear*
    —Ellie Harold
5   *Only one thing is more powerful than learning from experience, and
    that is not learning from experience!*—John M. Templeton

WEEK NINTEEN
1   *Make yourself necessary to the world and mankind will give you
    bread*—Ralph Waldo Emerson
2   *Happiness comes from spiritual wealth, not material wealth*
    —John M. Templeton
3   *Thoughts held in mind produce after their kind*—Charles Fillmore
4   *Progress requires change*—John M. Templeton
5   *Fortune knocks at the door of those who are prepared*—Anonymous

WEEK TWENTY
1   *A good reputation is more valuable than money*—Publilius Syrus
2   *To err is human, to forgive divine*—Alexander Pope
3   *Never do anything that you'll have to punish yourself for*
    —Anonymous
4   *Reverse the word "evil" and you have the word "live."*
    —Phinius P. Quimby
5   *He who has a "why" for which to live, can bear with almost any
    "how"*—Friedrich Nietzsche

WEEK TWENTY-ONE
1   *All that we are is the result of what we have thought*—Buddha
2   *Once a word has been allowed to escape, it cannot be recalled*
    —Wentworth Roscommon
3   *You have the most powerful weapons on earth—love and prayer*
    —John M. Templeton
4   *Remember, no one can make you feel inferior without your consent*
    —Eleanor Roosevelt
5   *No person was ever honored for what he received. Honor has been the
    reward for what he gave*—Calvin Coolidge

WEEK TWENTY-TWO
1   *Material progress needs entrepreneurs*—John M. Templeton
2   *As you are active in blessing others, they find their burdens easier to
    bear*—John M. Templeton
3   *Expect the best and your positive outlook opens the door to opportu-
    nity*—John M. Templeton
4   *When anger reigns, negative consequences occur*—Charles D. Lelly

5   *The wise person looks within his heart and finds eternal peace*
    —Hindu Proverb

WEEK TWENTY-THREE
1   *Preparedness is a step to success*—John M. Templeton
2   *You are on the road to success if you realize that failure is only a detour*—Corrie Ten Boom
3   *Thanksgiving leads to giving and forgiving, and to spiritual growth*
    —John M. Templeton
4   *There is no difficulty that enough love will not conquer*—Emmet Fox
5   *Self-control leads to success*—John M. Templeton

WEEK TWENTY-FOUR
1   *Your thoughts are like boomerangs*—Eileen Caddy
2   *You make yourself and others suffer just as much when you take offense as when you give offense*—Ken Keyes
3   *Little things mean a lot*—Edith Linderman
4   *To be upset over what you don't have is to waste what you do have*
    —Ken Keyes
5   *Honesty is the best policy*—Miguel de Cervantes

WEEK TWENTY-FIVE
1   *Your prayers can be answered by "Yes," but also by "No," and by "alternatives"*—Ruth Stafford Peale
2   *Healthy minds tend to cause healthy bodies and vice versa*
    —John M. Templeton
3   *Outward beauty is transient, but inner beauty lasting*
    —Seyyed Hossein Nasr
4   *A happy person is not a person in a certain set of circumstances, but rather a person with a certain set of attitudes*—Anonymous
5   *Help yourself by helping others*—John M. Templeton

WEEK TWENTY-SIX
1   *You create your own reality*—Jane Roberts
2   *A task takes as long as there is time to do it*—Parkinson's Law
3   *Often, a pat on the back works better than a kick in the pants*
    —William Juneau
4   *Give credit and help to all who have helped you*—John M. Templeton
5   *Thoughts can crystallize into habit and habit solidifies into circumstance*—Anonymous

WEEK TWENTY-SEVEN
1 *You can build your own heaven or hell on earth*—John M. Templeton
2 *A soft answer turns away wrath, but a harsh word stirs up anger*
   —Proverbs 15:1
3 *The pen is mightier than the sword*—E. G. Bulwer-Lytton
4 *Worry achieves nothing and wastes valuable time*
   —John M. Templeton
5 *The greatness is not in me; I am in the greatness*—Anonymous

WEEK TWENTY-EIGHT
1 *Laugh and the world laughs with you; weep and you weep alone*
   —Ella Wheeler Wilcox
2 *If nothing is ventured, nothing is gained*—Sir John Heywood
3 *Honesty is the first chapter in the book of wisdom*—Thomas Jefferson
4 *A man can fail many times, but he isn't a failure until he begins to
   blame others*—Ted Engstrom
5 *A soul without a high aim is like a ship without a rudder*
   —Eileen Caddy

WEEK TWENTY-NINE
1 *Joy provides assurance; envy brings loneliness*—John M. Templeton
2 *All sunshine makes a desert*—Oriental Proverb
3 *Whether you think you can or not, you are right*—Henry Ford
4 *The mind can make a heaven into a hell, or a hell into a heaven*
   —John Milton
5 *No man is free who is not master of himself*—Epictetus

WEEK THIRTY
1 *It is by forgetting self that one finds self*—St. Francis
2 *Leave no stone unturned*—Euripides
3 *What we focus on expands*—Arnold Patent
4 *As you think, so you are*—Charles Fillmore
5 *You choose the path you want to walk down*—John M. Templeton

WEEK THIRTY-ONE
1 *Destructive language tends to produce destructive results*
   —John M. Templeton
2 *Success feeds on itself and creates more success*—John M. Templeton
3 *Never put off until tomorrow what you can do today*
   —Lord Chesterfield
4 *Nothing is interesting if you are not interested*—John M. Templeton
5 *What is done is done*—William Shakespeare

WEEK THIRTY-TWO
1 *We can become bitter or better as a result of our experiences*
—Eric Butterworth
2 *Joy is not in things, but is in you*—John M. Templeton
3 *Misfortunes can be blessings*—John M. Templeton
4 *Happiness pursued, eludes; happiness given, returns*
—John M. Templeton
5 *Thoughts of doubt and fear are pathways to failure*—Brian Adams

WEEK THIRTY-THREE
1 *By their fruits, you shall know them*—Matthew 7:16
2 *Optimism has its roots in the abiding goodness*—Anonymous
3 *If you think you know it all, you are less likely to learn more*
—John M. Templeton
4 *We carry within us the wonders that we seek without us*
—Eric Butterworth
5 *The shadow of ignorance is fear*—J. Jelinek

WEEK THIRTY-FOUR
1 *You're either part of the problem or part of the solution*
—Eldridge Cleaver
2 *A loving person lives in a loving world*—Ken Keyes
3 *The borrower is a servant to the lender*—Proverbs 22:5.7
4 *Whatever you have, you must use it or lose it*—Henry Ford
5 *It's nice to be important, but it's more important to be nice*—John M.
Templeton

WEEK THIRTY-FIVE
1 *Those who seldom make mistakes seldom make discoveries*
—John M. Templeton
2 *The measure of a man's real character is what he would do if he would
never be found out*—Thomas Macaulay
3 *Change your mind to change your life*—John M. Templeton
4 *Progress and growth are impossible if you always do things the way
you've always done things*—Wayne Dyer
5 *It is more blessed to give than to receive*—Acts 20:35

WEEK THIRTY-SIX
1 *Holding onto grievances is a decision to suffer*—Gerald Jampolsky
2 *The seven deadly sins are: pride, lust, sloth, envy, anger, covetousness,
and gluttony*—St. Gregory
3 *Appearances are often deceiving*—Aesop

4   *Zeal is the inward fire of the soul that urges you onward toward your goal*—Charles Fillmore
5   *Minds are like parachutes—they only function when they are open*—Dick Sutphen

WEEK THIRTY-SEVEN
1   *You are more defined by what comes out of your mouth than by what goes in*—Anonymous
2   *The journey of a thousand miles begins with the first step*—Lao Tzu
3   *The dark of night is not the end of the world*—Anonymous
4   *Love conquers all things*—Virgil
5   *Count your blessings every day and they will grow and multiply like well-tended plants*—William Juneau

WEEK THIRTY-EIGHT
1   *You never really lose until you stop trying*—Mike Ditka
2   *Everyone should keep in reserve an alternate plan for livelihood*—John M. Templeton
3   *If you are facing in the right direction, all you need to do is keep walking*—Buddhist Proverb
4   *The unknown is not unknowable, and is vastly greater than the known*—John M. Templeton
5   *Forgiveness benefits both the giver and the receiver*—John M. Templeton

WEEK THIRTY-NINE
1   *Humility opens the door to progress*—John M. Templeton
2   *Your dreams can come true when you activate them*—John M. Templeton
3   *Work is love made visible*—Kahlil Gibran
4   *For every effect, there is a cause*—Hermetic Principle
5   *Those who do good do well*—John M. Templeton

WEEK FORTY
1   *Focus on where you want to go, instead of where you have been*—John M. Templeton
2   *You get back what you give out*—John M. Templeton
3   *Thanksgiving opens the door to spiritual growth*—John M. Templeton
4   *The more love we give, the more love we have left*—John M. Templeton
5   *Every useful life is a ministry*—John M. Templeton

Statement on Humility Theology

by Mark Richardson and Judith Marchand
as edited by John Marks Templeton on December 13, 1995

Objectives

An objective of Humility Theology is to encourage progress in spiritual information and research especially by interpreting diverse kinds of evidence from scientific investigations. Humility Theology, through inquiry into the observable world, presses toward information regarding matters of ultimacy.

Humility Theology encourages the idea that spiritual understanding and information continues to increase—human understanding should not be fixed and unchanging. Thus our knowledge is provisional; claims to possessing the full truth are unintentionally egotistical. Within this flux of time Humility Theology pursues evidence about spiritual information and Ultimate Reality (which some major religions call God), including design, purpose, love, and prayer. Time-honoured beliefs should be open to supplementation, improvement, or revision in view of continuous discoveries or unfolding of God's purposes.

The main purpose of the John Templeton Foundation is to encourage the top one-tenth of 1 percent of people and thereby encourage all people to think that progress in spiritual information is possible, desirable, can be done and will be done. Methods of statistics and of science may produce rapid progress in spiritual information as already produced in medicine and electronics. That progress in spiritual information can be enormously beneficial in accordance with God's purposes for all his children everywhere. As in other sciences the benefits are often unforeseen. More and more information (if verified by statistical or experimental evidence or other methods of science) can be recognized worldwide promptly after each discovery and thereby provide an increasing supplement to the wonderful revelations of all ancient scriptures and prophets, which have been so beneficial for thousands of years.

Spiritual information can be, should be, and will be rapidly increasing and accelerating. New information verified by statistics or experimental evidence or methods of science can be accepted worldwide quickly, as it is now in other sciences.

Methods

Humility Theology interprets modern scientific developments in regard to what they might reveal about spiritual principles and the nature and the ways of God. In addition, where appropriate, it seeks to apply the hypothetical-deductive methods of the sciences to examination of spiritual data. Often this can be done by posing concepts in a testable mode, reflecting the provisionality, incompleteness, and fallibility of human utterances about spiritual reality.

Some methods of Humility Theology can be inferential. Reasonable concepts about unseen realities beyond our observation can be drawn from evidence based in those phenomena which are open to observation, experience, or analysis.

Attitudes

Humility Theology begins with the assumption that, because of our finitude in the face of the vastness of all reality, human knowledge about God, and about the world the scientist explores, should be regarded as very limited, and tentatively held.

Nevertheless, through the rigors of statistical, experimental, or other scientific methods of inquiry, there can be progress in our spiritual information. Toward this end, Humility Theology encourages an open-mindedness toward any new ideas, a respectful manner of engagement with those who hold different views, and a non-dogmatic style of presenting ideas.

Finally, Humility Theology encourages an attitude among theologians and scientists of respect for all religious traditions, openness to new theological insights based on the broadest possible range of human learning, testing and experience, and reverence toward God as the unlimited creative spirit and only Ultimate Reality. How little we know—how eager to learn.

Postscript

The Templeton Foundations encourage progress in spiritual information and research. We have unlimited admiration for the wonderful benefits from all ancient scriptures, revelations, and prophets; but accelerating progress in spiritual information can result from experiments and research using methods of sciences.

We use the word information to include data history, principles, and concepts. We use the word spiritual to include those realities which lie beyond the visible, tangible, and temporary. We use the word spiritual to include love, joy, peace, patience, kindness, goodness, faithfulness, gentleness, self-control, self-sacrifice, honesty, reliability, humility, curiosity, purpose, creativity, progress, ethics, giving, forgiving, and thanksgiving.

Appendix J

Humility Theology Questions

from John Marks Templeton

1. Can science research increase more than a hundredfold earth's information about reality, timeless and limitless, which some people call God?
2. If we do not understand why matter exists or light or gravity, could that mean that reality is vastly more complex than humans yet comprehend, just as our ancestors did not comprehend television, germs, atoms, or galaxies?
3. Have the major religions been held back by an unconscious concept that God is somehow separate from reality, a sort of wise old king as in the ancient story of Adam and Eve?
4. Has human ego caused us to visualize a God in human terms?
5. Is God larger than a single race or planet?
6. Have human concepts of God always been too small? Too anthropomorphic?
7. Is God timeless and unlimited? Omnipresent? Increasingly creative?
8. If each branch of science is showing that creation is vastly wider and more complex than comprehended two millennia ago or even just one century ago, does this reveal a Creator even more worthy of adoration?
9. Can our worship increase as we learn more of the timeless limitless God?
10. Will this comprehension of a larger, greater Creator continue? Will this continue to speed up?
11. Will accelerating discoveries reveal multitudes of new mysteries?
12. Does recent science research show us that the invisible is vastly larger and more varied than the visible?
13. Is the invisible more than one hundred times larger and more varied than the visible?
14. Is the visible only a tiny, temporary manifestation of reality?

15. Can anything ever be separate from God?
16. Is God the only reality?
17. Is God all of me and I a tiny part of him?
18. Why are earthlings being created?
19. Am I an expression or agent of God in love and creativity?
20. Does God live in you and you in him?
21. Can heaven be the result of prayer, worship, usefulness, and giving, forgiving, thanksgiving, and unlimited love?
22. Should we be enthusiastic and diligent to discover more about God?
23. Is it likely that earthlings are the ultimate?
24. Can there be intelligences surrounding us yet not comprehensible to us? What are the chances that such creatures already exist?
25. What are the chances that varieties of creatures already exist not yet comprehensible by us?
26. Is it likely that on the planets of more than one hundred billion stars in our galaxy and one hundred billion other galaxies, there are manifestations of God's creativity not yet imagined by earthlings and maybe more advanced than we?
27. Could living creatures on earth only ten million years ago conceive of present human intelligence?
28. Is it likely that many realities in and around us are not comprehensible by humans, just as electronics and subatomics were not comprehensible only one century ago?
29. Do the discoveries by science just since Galileo about realities not previously comprehended by humans resemble the discoveries about realities that followed the development of eyes by the first creature?
30. Should this cause us to worship a God larger than comprehended by the ancients?
31. Are there multiplying evidences of purpose in the universe and in creativity?
32. Does humanity have purpose?
33. Why is humanity being created?
34. Can we discover more about God's purposes?
35. How can we learn to be helpers in God's purposes?
36. Is science research, which has flourished for only the latest 1 percent of 1 percent of human history, still in its infancy?
37. If human information has multiplied more than one hundredfold in only two centuries, will that progress accelerate, so that in the year 2200 information can be more than ten thousand times as great as in 1800?

38. Can progress continue to accelerate?
39. Is it likely that by accelerating progress, more than half of what is taught as science today will become obsolete in only one century?
40. Can human concepts of God expand even more rapidly than science reveals reality?
41. By devoting one-tenth of all science research to the discovery of new spiritual information, can the benefits be even greater than from other science research?
42. Should we listen carefully, thoughtfully, and gratefully to everyone's concepts of God and God's purposes for humanity?
43. Do we know as little about God in whom we live as a clam knows about the ocean in which it lives and about submarines in that same ocean?
44. If a wave is a tiny temporary manifestation of the ocean of which it is a part, does that resemble our relation to God?
45. Can all the wonderfully beneficial ancient scriptures be supplemented more than one hundredfold by science research for spiritual information and verification?
46. Is all science research further information about God?
47. Is it egotistical to think that humans can ever devise a "theory of everything"?
48. Do we now comprehend more than one hundred times as much about God's creativity as humans understood just one thousand years ago?
49. Is it possible that research in genetics or other sciences can accelerate progress of human intelligence?
50. Is helping in God's creativity a way to express our thankfulness?
51. Can prayer, worship, and service to others help each of us to discover more of the nature of God?
52. Does Humility Theology mean more questions than answers?
53. Does free competition of diverse spiritual concepts accelerate progress in religion, ideas, and human welfare?
54. Is free and loving competition part of God's plan for progress, productivity, and prosperity for his children?
55. Can science research reduce conflict between religions?
56. Are there some laws from the great religions for happy and fruitful life, which can be tested by science research and studied and researched in schools worldwide?
57. Can some universities encourage and train some students to make careers in Humility Theology research?

Notes

CHAPTER 1

1. J. M. Templeton and R. L. Herrmann, *The God Who Would Be Known* (San Francisco: Harper & Row, 1989), 5.
2. Timothy Ferris, *Coming of Age in The Milky Way* (New York: William Morrow, 1988), 383.
3. J. M. Templeton, *The Humble Approach* (New York: Continuum Publishing Company, 1995), 18-20.
4. Ibid., 34–36.
5. R. S. Cole-Turner, *An Unavoidable Challenge: Our Church in an Age of Science and Technology* (: United Church Board for Homeland Ministries, 1992), 20.
6. Templeton, *The Humble Approach*, 39–41.

CHAPTER 2

1. John M. Templeton, *The Humble Approach*. (New York: Continuum Publishing Company, 1995), 118–121.
2. Ibid., 121–122.
3. William Proctor, *The Templeton Prizes* (New York: Doubleday, 1983), 2.
4. J. M. Templeton, *The Humble Approach*, 122.
5. Ibid., 125–126.
6. Ibid., 122.
7. Ibid., 123.
8. Ibid., 123.
9. Ibid., 123.
10. John M. Templeton, Letter to Father Robert Sirico at the Acton Institute for the Study of Religion and Liberty, Grand Rapids, Michigan, July 5, 1991.

11. J. M. Templeton, *The Humble Approach*, 123.
12. Ibid., 123.
13. John M. Templeton, "The Laws of Life," *Plus* 40, no. 3 (April 1989).
14. John M. Templeton, *Discovering The Laws of Life* (New York: Continuum, 1994), 3–7.

CHAPTER 3
1. John M. Templeton, *Evidence of Purpose* (New York: Continuum, 1994), 7–9.
2. Paul M. Davies, *The Mind of God* (New York: Simon & Schuster, 1992), 226–227.
3. David Wilcox, "How Blind the Watchmaker?" in *Evidence of Purpose*, ed. J. M. Templeton (New York: Continuum, 1994), 176–177.
4. Fred Hoyle, "The Universe: Past and Present Reflections," in *University of Cardiff Report* 70 (1981): 43.
5. Davies, *The Mind of God*, 229.
6. Ibid., 232.
7. Russell Stannard, *Grounds for Reasonable Belief* (Edinburgh: Scottish Academic Press, 1989), 169.

CHAPTER 7
1. John M. Templeton, *The Humble Approach*, 1–2.
2. Ibid., 6.
3. Ibid., 32–33.
4. Robert Sollod, "A Hollow Curriculum," *The Chronicle of Higher Education* 38, no. 2 (March 18, 1992): A60.
5. Stephen Cain, "U-M Studies Ways to Instill Values," *The Ann Arbor News*, 27 October 1994.

CHAPTER 11
1. William Proctor, *The Templeton Prizes* (New York: Doubleday, 1983), 62–63.
2. "The Principle of Maximum Pessimism," *Forbes*, 16 January 1995, 68.
3. Gary Moore, *Ten Golden Rules for Financial Success* (Grand Rapids: Zondervan, 1996), 19.
4. Burton D. Morgan, "How Sir John Saved My Life," John Templeton 80th Birthday Memory Book, 1992.

CHAPTER 12

1. R. L. Herrmann, "Professor Paul Davies Is 1995 Templeton Prize Winner," *Progress in Theology* 3, no. 3 (September 1995): 1.
2. R. L. Herrmann, "The Center's Research Program," *Progress in Theology* 1, no. 1 (March 1993): 3.
3. R. L. Herrmann, "Center for Humility Theology Renamed Humility Theology Information Center," *Progress in Theology* 1, no. 3 (1993): 1.
4. R. L. Herrmann, "Benjamin Franklin Medal Presented to Sir John Templeton," *Progress in Theology* 3, no. 1 (1995): 1, 3.
5. R. L. Herrmann, "Ceremony Marks Completion of Westminster Abbey Restoration," *Progress in Theology* 4, no. 1 (March 1966)
6. Wilbert Forker, ed., "Foreword," in *The Future Agenda* (Edinburgh: The Hanover Press, 1992),

CHAPTER 13

1. Robert L. Herrmann, "How Large is God? How Deep is Reality?," in *How Large is God?*, ed. John M. Templeton (Philadelphia, Pennsylvania: Templeton Foundation Press, 1997), 217–250.
2. John M. Templeton and Robert L. Herrmann, *The God Who Would Be Known* (San Francisco: Harper and Row, 1989), 121–122.
3. John M. Templeton, ed., "Introduction," in *Evidence of Purpose,* (New York: Continuum, 1994), 11.
4. "Science and Spiritual Quest Program Moving Ahead," *Progress in Theology* 4, no. 4 (December 1996): 8.
5. *Progress in Theology* 5, no. 1 (January/February 1997): 1, 6.
6. *Progress in Theology* 4, no. 4 (December 1996): 6.

Index